# My Childhood Heaven

# My Childhood Heaven

AGNES ROBERTSON

The Pentland Press
Edinburgh–Cambridge–Durham–USA

First published in 1994
by The Pentland Press Ltd
1 Hutton Close
South Church
Bishop Auckland
Durham

British Library
Cataloguing in Publication Data

A catalogue record for this book
is available from the British Library

ISBN 1-85821-258-8

Typeset by Carnegie Publishing Ltd., 18 Maynard St., Preston
Printed and bound by Antony Rowe Ltd., Chippenham

# My Childhood Heaven

THE unexpected, like miracles, still happens and I have experienced both, the unexpected recently leaving me very amused. As the old saying goes, a good hearty laugh is often a better tonic than the best of medicines, and so it was with me.

The very thought that I could write a book! Of course my friend was joking, so I thought, until other friends, visiting from England, suddenly said that I should write a book. Now thought I, stunned for a moment, have I taken on a professional look? Who would not agree with me if they knew I had left school as the dunce in the family. However, that is another story.

I am no chicken either, and am preparing daily to be worthy of my "Eternal Home" in glory, and not thinking of writing a book. All would also agree with me once they knew I was born on 24th June, 1907, in unusual and unexpected happenings – a thunder storm that covered and destroyed all the beauty and perfumes of the lovely roses in full bloom round our cottage door.

Life when I was young was entirely different from the very sad life so many people have to live through nowadays, especially the children. What childhood have they with so many evils, etc., going on?

Still, I must not dwell on such sad happenings. However, one thing I will say is that, from my very own point of view, the TV was one of the worst things to have come into any home. Even if it has good points, that does not make up for the filth and evil shown. So, as often the subject now is war or the state of the world as a whole, I then refer back to my long past happy childhood, hence the interest for me to write a book.

After giving the persuasion of my friends much thought, I decided that to write a book would not be such a bad idea after all, as going over the past and reliving my childhood onwards should give me much pleasure, now that my energy keeps getting less and I have to rest so much. Also, the very mistakes I made could give amusement to any reader – should they only be my own younger relations.

What really decided me to write a book was my good samaritan friend, as I call her. Once a week she takes me up to the long-term hospital wing, where my sister has been a patient for the last four years. She then goes on to do our weekly shopping. After having spent the afternoon with my sister, I return home to find my grocery box in my small vestibule.

One particular afternoon, on coming in, I see this large plastic bag, resting beside my grocery box, with Woolworths printed across it in large letters. Curiosity getting the better of me, I just had to have a peep before I could open the glass door and take it all into the house. Oh, such a queer feeling came over me which I could not explain, even to myself, for there I spied the largest jotter ever, bolted well into its strong, red battleship-like cover, also a small case of pens.

Oh, Agnes, I said to myself, Mary has lifted your anchor so you must set sail, and to have a happy and successful voyage I must take the good Lord as my Captain. Then, who knows, I may sail into a pleasant harbour with a finished book an enjoyable read.

I was born on a small farm on the Isle of Mull, the fourth child of the family. Having two girls then a boy, mother, I was often told, looked forward to a second boy. Alas, seemingly, it was putting it mildly to say I disappointed her. However, towards the latter end of her life, I made up to her for any disappointment I caused. I was the one who stayed single to care for my parents, the done thing in those far gone days, when always a daughter stayed single and at home to care for the parents. If no daughter, then a son generally stayed dutifully, but if there was no family, there was always someone near that did the caring.

I was the one at hand to care for our nice, kind neighbour who sadly died at the young age of thirty-seven, leaving three children at school. Fortunately, the father soon re-married – a capable girl and friend of the family, who proved to be an excellent, caring mother to the young children.

My father did not own the farm, but managed it for an older uncle who was at sea, sailing abroad. I have no recollection of my childhood on Mull, as I was only a year old when, as needs must, we had to uplift our roots. The reason for this move was that my two sisters were now of school age. My eldest sister had been held back until the second reached school age, there being only eleven months difference in their ages. Also there was no school within easy reach of the farm.

In those far gone days the ways of obtaining employment were far different in every way, as I suppose were most things from today. Twice a year, in May and November, there was what was known as a feeing market held in our town of Oban, when those looking for employees and others seeking employment attended.

Father, going to attend the fair was, while on the steamer to Oban, fortunate to have met the factor from the nearby estate of Ardtornish, on the mainland of Morvern. He was looking for a shepherd, so before Oban was reached, they came to very suitable terms. With a good school only fifteen minutes walk from home, there we remained for the next fifty years.

I then, looking round with so many happy and sad memories, had to uplift my roots and say goodbye to the old home after the death of mother, who lived for ten years after father. My father's unexpected death, in his seventy-second year, was caused through him over exerting himself while helping a neighbour with his cattle.

From Mull to the mainland of Morvern was a short sail of half-an-hour, where at the pier, known as Lochaline, we were met by our new neighbour to transport us to our new home via a horse and cart – this being the only form of transport in those far gone days, except for the wealthy and millionaires such as our new boss. How I still remember driving in such a beautiful, glittering carriage, with an equally beautiful horse trotting as if trained as a soldier.

My first recollection of our new home, when I think I would be about three years old, was when an aunt and uncle came on holiday, bringing my brother a little speedboat. What joy that little boat brought us, one on each side of a small pond, winding up the boat and sending it speeding to each other. If they brought me a gift, I have no recollection of it, nor have I any recollection of how long the little boat lasted.

Sharing our tender growing years with God's wonderful creatures of all kinds and sizes, farm animals, birds, and endless butterflies of countless colours which we loved chasing gave us much pleasure, as did trying to find the singing grasshoppers and other insects playing in the warm grass, but all evading us.

There was the beauty of countless wild flowers growing so plentifully in all sorts of places among the equally lovely green grass which felt so nice as we roamed about on our bare feet during those long, glorious summers.

Young as I was, I always saw God in everything, whither the humblest flowers such as buttercups and daisies, or the young lambs earlier in the spring. The young calves put out on tether for the first time to enjoy the wonderful world and sunshine from their more darkened sheds where they generally lived from when they were born usually in February or March. No wonder father had to tether them on a long rope, as with their dancing and jumping for sheer joy they could easily have come to grief. There were the young chicks, and their proud mother hen forever clucking and scraping in the grass to train her lovely brood how to find tasty insects. Also there were the young pups, which we adored, being so very playful.

I remember later on in years, when we as a family were grown up and mother fancied a small dog of her own, having at last some time to herself after such a long and very busy life. She got a small cairn terrier pup, and no one need tell me that animals aren't intelligent creatures, who can do anything but speak. Even if they don't speak, they can always make one understand what they mean.

However, I am jumping the queue, as it were, so back to my childhood.

Our home was built on what must have been, at one time, a large green field. My reason for thinking this is, that before our time, it was a shooting lodge before being converted into two dwelling houses for workers. The places round about were so well laid out, but now given back to flowers. My favourites, which I still remember so well, were special, beautiful, white lilies, whose name I never learned. Their wonderful perfume still lingers with me when I remember them, as I do equally, the lovely red roses that grew along the banks of an equally lovely river that flowed to the left side of the house, with such clear water and pebbles all washed rounded with no rugged edges. The purity of the clean, clear river – it came down for miles – was due to the fact that there was nothing to pollute it from the lonely hills.

The roses, like the lilies, had such a beautiful perfume which reached us before we reached the roses. What did puzzle me was that although some of the roses would be awash at times after heavy rain, they were never spoiled and came up in all their beauty once the river went down.

Looking back, how entirely different the whole world and life is today from those far gone times. Each season also so entirely different and so very beautiful. To talk about it now seems an unreal dream, but we read that the prophets foretold that the days would come when their would be little difference between the seasons' weather, and who can but agree that such is true today.

In the past, from April until early October, we would cast off our boots and thoroughly enjoy the freedom of running about in our bare feet-which seemed to harden during those lovely long months.

Sunday, of course, was different. That was known as God's special day. He gave His people to rest from their labours and remember all His blessings. We were to respect it and give Him thanks by going to Church and Sunday School. Also, of course, we respected Him and His day by dressing special. I remember how proud we were when dressed up, something like all the young animals jumping and dancing about for sheer joy.

Our Sunday best comprised lovely dresses, straw hats with a ring of large daisies round the crown of straw and its broad brim shading our eyes from the sun. Also lovely pale blue and pink ribbons setting off our hair with a huge bow, our hair having been washed and pleated after our bath on Saturday night. Then, when all the pleats were undone before going to church, we thought ourselves beautiful with such nice clean, wavy hair and all dressed up.

One thing we were not comfortable in was our brown, light canvas shoes and white socks, but we suffered gladly as it was

God's special day. The reason for our discomfort was that we were barefoot all week in the summer months.

Going to church meant a walk of five miles, both ways, which we always enjoyed and never felt tired. My brother and I were always finding things of interest and falling behind, until father's call brought us running to catch up. We always liked passing the different houses, although they were few, as there was something different about them all. One, I remember, had turkeys, so we always loathed to leave that house.

In church of course, we never talked, not even in whispers, as God would not like it. We found our interest in the people coming in with such respect, and it was nice to see how different they all were in their various dresses.

On getting home from church, with a huge appetite, mother always had our special favourite, and easily prepared, Sunday lunch of bacon, eggs and fried onions. Our breakfast was always well-cooked porridge and a cup of tea with a scone and fresh butter which, like most things, was all mother's making. I do remember she was wonderfully clever, and never idle. How I truly do believe that she is very happy enjoying her long well-earned rest. Even when she sat in the evenings, it was to knit, sew or mend for her large brood, which had grown to four more boys after her disappointment over me being a girl.

While her hands were so busy, we would be strung around her as she always spent her time doubly well, by telling lovely and interesting stories, often Bible ones. This was to our advantage later in life by helping us to try be the children she always prayed we would be. That is my reason for knowing she is blessed and happy with God in our "Eternal Home", where I, like the rest of the family not already gone, look forward one day to a joyous reunion.

After our enjoyable meal and a quiet rest, it was off to Sunday School, another lovely 1½ mile walk to our country hall, a walk always much enjoyed. Having to pass a small garden with gooseberry bushes, all laden with red and yellow berries, brought an awful longing and temptation for us children. We could not understand why the old couple in the cottage never ate them, in fact they seemed to rot as we watched them with longing eyes and watering mouths.

On returning home it would be porridge again, as for breakfast, then father would take out the family Bible for our evening lesson. After this we would prepare for bed where we would untie our hair ribbons, fold them nicely and put them into our Bibles. The rest of our Sunday clothes would be properly laid aside.

Strange to say, I never remember wet Sundays during those long gone times but, as I have stated, we had lovely, long summers and I recall we more or less lived outdoors. It was a job for mother to get us in and washed for bed.

# Summer School Holidays

I HAVE no recollection of starting school, but what I do recall was that one of the older girls loved sitting me on the teacher's garden wall, and tipping me down and up. Once she tipped me too far and dropped me into the garden, smashing the lovely flowers, so that was an end to that.

Our first excitement of the holidays was the sheep clipping. The shepherds had a very early breakfast of eggs, fried oatcake and home cured-bacon. This bacon was preserved specially from our winter supply which, I remember, was hung on hooks from the high ceiling of our kitchen once it had been cured in a large barrel, from the kill in November. Mother melted down all the lard, this amount lasting all winter, for frying her home-made oatcakes which tasted so delicious with the bacon when our eggs were so scarce.

Before the gatherings, the men would close off as stretch of green in front of our house by wooden gates, or flakes as they were called, tied together by wooden stakes hammered into the ground. This formed an enclosure for the sheep, when clipped, until all the work was finished and the sheep ready to return to the hills. At the far end of this enclosure were sheds, one with seats for the shepherds' clipping, the others at the back held the sheep.

I think the men numbered twelve and several had different jobs to perform. Two would fetch the sheep that were to be clipped. One had charge of seeing to a fire, which to me seemed to be in a bucket with holes round it, into which were put markers for branding the sheep when clipped. Over this fire, hanging on a swivel, was a pot of pitch or tar that the man put the marker into once he took it out of the fire. It was this tar mark that enabled each shepherd to know his own sheep once out on the hills. Other men would be trimming and rolling the fleece, as the wool was called after being taken off the sheep.

Where we children got most of our fun was on a tall stand which always stood outside the sheds. This, I would say, was about seven feet high and made of thick, round wooden poles, two firmly bedded in the ground and one across the top, on which rested a ladder. A large strong bag was firmly hung up into which was put a few of the rolled fleece. A man then stepped inside the bag, with only his hand to be seen at first, taking hold of the fleece and packing them tight. When the bag was filled, it was sewn before being removed. We children did have fun playing on the bags as they grew in number.

It was a very busy time for the shepherds as they worked long hours, going to the hills at 3.30 a.m. so as to gather the sheep before they started to roam. It was a lovely sight seeing 5 to 6 hundred sheep coming down the hill, kept in a fairly straight line by the shepherds' wise dogs. Each man had two collie dogs, and how these dogs enjoyed their work.

Once the sheep were safely penned, the men then went indoors for a rest and their porridge. There was no rush to get back out as the sheep were generally wet with dew and they had to be thoroughly dried, once the sun came out, before they could be clipped. The clipping took three to four weeks, then the men left for the further end of the estate to do the sheep from the hills there, so we didn't have them back home until the work was finished, with the exception of weekends.

Estates were united through marriage hence the reason for their being so large. Our part was known as Ardtornish, and the other part, Fuinary. The men were well housed and fed during such busy times, as one of the wives in both places did the needful work, the estate supplying them with plenty of mutton and all other food. We only had father with us for breakfast which he found more convenient while working at the home end.

As a family we seemed to pair off by age, my two sisters, then my brother and I, and we seldom seemed to separate, until our schooldays, when we chummed up with neighbours boys and girls of about our own age. Then things changed. The boys, often anxious to get away on their own, played endless tricks to do so. This particular time they were the farmers and we were the animals – two cows – we were then taken into the byre and, for some reason I cannot now remember, our hair was interwoven by pleating. Then we were taken up to the cows' food trough and left there to moo while the farmers went to fetch us some hay. Sadly, all our mooings never brought the farmers back and there we were, stuck together, until we decided that enough was enough and made our way slowly home to get released.

Sometimes in the evenings my brother would like to go fishing, with home-made rod and worms on bent pins. Of course I always went with him for company, even although I was miserable sitting on the bank of the river being almost eaten alive by midges. Of course all of this was for nothing, as he never would catch his longed-for fish.

Once he got his boy pal he didn't want my company, so I was chased home. Feeling very miserable, I decided I'd go fishing on my own. To make a rod, I searched around and the best I could get was a small, twisted, rotten root of a tree from the river side. To this I tied a string with twisted pin and worm, then into the water it went while I bent on my knees and clasped my hands together and prayed: "Please God, give me a wee fish." On going to lift my rod, what excitement, for God did send me my wee fish – a minnow about one inch long. I was so excited, running home so fast, to put my fish into mother's tub, which was always kept full of water, that I seemed to keep tripping and taking longer to get home. The minnow, of course, only floated in the tub water. Still, God did answer a wee girl's prayer, and how, in old age, that incident remains very clear. What is also as joyous, is that I can in all truth say that God has answered several prayers since, and all wonderful miracles. Some I may write about later in my book.

Schooldays do not hold many memories for me, although school was certainly a lovely building and the flower garden was beautiful. Yet as in every generation, and even now is no exception, religion always caused some sadness, as it did in our school although there was never any complaint. The reason was that our form of worship was of the Church of Scotland, hence I was so often unable to concentrate on my lessons as teacher would often say and do things that were very hurtful for young children. I remember she was always very charming to grown-ups, as she was to my parents, and father never wanted to complain for fear of matters being made worse. Of course, some children were more sensitive than others, and I felt hurt when I'd see her treating others in a hurtful way.

One thing that I do recollect is that in the river near our school, was a large salmon pool, and we were allowed out to see the gents and their ghillies when they would be scringing. This was most interesting and lovely sight, when the nets were being dragged to the land with about forty to fifty salmon jumping to escape, their bright scaled bodies shining like silver.

Mother, as we got older and my new young brother started moving about, decided that I must spend much of my time playing and looking after him, as my other sisters now made to do other useful home-work. I didn't think mother ever really forgave dad for not allowing her to take her home help, a nice girl of eighteen years, to our new home. He said it would look out of place since he was only now to be a shepherd. So Tilda, as she was called, went to help another aunt living in Mull. Like lots of other young girls who came from poor homes in Glasgow, after leaving school, Tilda spent all her life with my cousins, even dying with them in old age.

Mother used to tell us how happy Tilda was looking after us all day, which left mother free for other work. No wonder she lamented the loss of Tilda when she got four more boys after me. Besides Tilda, she lamented not being allowed to take quite a few things, the most useful being our pram – father saying it was too stylish.

At that time I was still a babe in the pram, so I do not remember it. In later life I was told that it was white with brass fittings, and was picked and sent to mother in Mull by a cousin living in Glasgow. What I do remember was that we were reduced to a second-hand pram someone was finished with and that it also did for my four younger brothers.

Our new home was in a very quiet place and mother always was much too busy to ever leave home, unless it was for a day's outing to Oban in the summer. For that day she had to be up with the larks, as the old saying goes for she had to go out and take the cows in to milk. Often they would be quite a distance from the home, and they would still be resting as the wise animals knew themselves when it would be near milking time, and would always make for home. After mother brought home the milk and saw to all the morning work, she then had a five-mile walk to catch the 9 o'clock steamer. Life was no picnic in those days, but everyone seemed happy and content, as living in such a lovely country place and with so many other added blessings, there was no need of complaints or for holidays.

Mother, when we as a family thought and talked about it in

later years, must have been a wonderful person to get through such endless work while eight of us were growing up, especially when it is known that in those far gone days nothing was as easy as it is in life today. She baked and cooked all the food we ate, potatoes and porridge the least of her cooking, even bread was never bought, while also cooking for the animals.

We certainly had a lovely, large and roomy home, but no modern gadgets. All cooking and heating of water was done on the large kitchen range, and that had to be kept well stoked. It always seemed to be covered with pots and pans, for when we were fed then the animal pans were put on. The flues had to be thoroughly cleaned once a week for the oven to work properly.

Father liked the calves born February or early March, so all hot drinks for the cows had to be heated on the range, for we had no hot water in the house until several years later, when we also got a proper bathroom. We then had lashings of boiling water without any extra cost from the range, no wonder my parents often lamented the wasted heat going up the chimney as the large range roared.

As for electricity, both parents were gone to their "Eternal Home" as we as a family scattered in homes of our own, long before electricity reached most of the Highlands. However, we certainly through time moved up from the candles and ordinary paraffin lamps to more modern kinds, which were very much of an improvement, although they meant extra work to start up. They also, like the old type, had to be filled and cleaned daily.

As I stated previously, nothing came easily in the past years, and for washing the wash-house boiler fire had to be lit early for the water to boil to get through such a huge load of clothes once a week. This was in itself a hard day's work, and like the kitchen range, it had to be kept well stoked. All the washing had then to be carried out and hung on lines to dry, collected when dry – more hard work – before the ironing and pressing of different garments. This was no easy task either, as iron bolts were put into the midst of the fire and heated until red hot, before being put into the iron holder – a very hot and tiring job. As each bolt cooled, it was returned to the fire and the other bolt was taken out.

Even the clothes were very cumbersome compared with the clothes of today, being so much more difficult to iron, while the heat from the well-stoked fire and hot irons sapped so much of one's strength. All the long, fancy topped stockings father wore, mother knitted, as in those days men wore breeches, except on Sundays when going to church, then they wore clerical grey, long-trousered suits. We children also wore her knitted socks in winter and early spring, before we discarded our boots for the summer. No wonder it was when she got us all to bed, that she would clean the house.

The range was dreadfully hard work to keep clean, a horrid paste known as blacklead being brushed over the grate, and when dry, brushed off with the dust off it going up one's nose. The steel parts were just as hard to polish by using plenty of elbow grease while rubbing them with sandpaper.

Thinking back, as I write this today, with everything so simple, a case of pressing buttons, etc., I reflect on the sad state of the whole world through evils of all kinds with greed of material gains and money causing such selfishness. All the best things in life that really matter are God given, free to us all. It does make me think that our hard life of the past was the best after all, as people were more content with their lot – not making a God the love of money, which is very often the root of most evils.

On one of mother's outings to Oban, taking my eldest sister with her, unknowingly they were in contact with someone having had scarlet fever, and it ended up that we as a family all caught it, and had to be isolated. A young nurse, on finishing her training in Glasgow, came to care for us so the germ didn't spread to anyone else. I must have been about four years old as I remember the time well, and it really was not a bad type of fever.

When the nurse had finished with us, she went as district nurse to a small village on the Isle of Mull, known as Dervaig. She remained there for the rest of her life, having married and settled down, giving birth to two children. She always kept in touch with us and would return to us on holidays with the children, as we would to them, so it was a fair exchange. In those days, people more or less only holidayed with relations or friends, as money was generally scarce.

This friendship lasted for life and I have watched the different members go to their Eternal rest. We as a family, are now slipping away from the different homes, so widely scattered about, leaving in turn, their families to carry on, with the exception of myself, having remained the spinster aunt.

Both my parents passed away very unexpectedly. Father, at seventy-two, was helping a neighbour to move animals to a new home, and over-taxed his strength, from which he never recovered and died of pneumonia. Mother lived ten years after father and died in her eightieth year from a leak in the valve of her heart, minutes after her doctor had taken her blood pressure.

Shortly after her passing, I went for a quiet week's holiday to Ardgour, and sitting by the shore of Loch Lynnhe, having a picnic lunch, my thoughts drifted to what the future held for me. I was just saying to myself, Agnes, you are alone now for the first time in your life, with no one requiring your help, when suddenly, without warning, the still, clear inward voice of God said, you are not alone, I am with you. Honestly, sitting there in the silence and beauty of the summer's day all around,

I certainly felt God's presence, and what a wonderful glow of happiness it brought me in my loneliness. I can truly say that I have felt his presence with me ever since.

My next recollections were of the 1914 war, with its ration cards and restrictions, but having the croft, with plenty of fields to grow food and also the animals, we were never hungry. In fact, my parents were able to share quite a lot with some less fortunate neighbours.

I also remember that, young as we were, we had to work very hard on getting home from school. It was a case of changing into glad rags as each season brought its own type of work.

During the winter we would be helping with the firewood, and once into the nice, dry April weather, we would be up in the peat moss spreading out the peats as father cut them. Over the weeks, as they dried, they had to be turned and stacked. There was then the garden work, and later on, the hay and corn with us often having to work late after the sun set. It was real agony with the midges, but there was no escaping until the work was finished.

Then, as autumn came round, it was into the potato field with our backs bent all day lifting the potatoes – a job we all dreaded.

It was different in the spring when the potatoes were being planted. That was a busy day as the estate ploughman, with his plough and team of horses, along with other workmen, came up to help father get the work done. All the men were especially well fed, getting tea with oatcake and cheese, and scones with butter and jam, sent out to them before starting work. They all came into the house for a good lunch, while the horses were also loosed and fed. All got a glass of scotch, which was bought in specially for them to get them through the long busy day, to start their lunch. Afternoon tea was then sent out to the field, so no wonder they all looked forward to the Acharn potato planting.

Apart from our own home-work, we were often sent on Saturdays and holidays, three miles up a glen to help two sisters living alone. The husband of one of them had been taken to the war and she had no family of her own, this being the reason why her spinster sister went to live with her.

The autumn also saw us busy gathering everything indoors for the winter. Father took home the peats and wood, packing them neatly in the sheds, and what a grand sight the packed sheds looked, us knowing that we were well supplied for winter fuel, coal being an unheard of luxury for us then. Then there was the hay to be carted home and put into the barn above the byre.

Quite a lot of potatoes were also carted home and put into a shed, the stone floor of which was well covered with dry bracken to protect the potatoes from the keen frost. What the shed could not take was bedded, also in dry bracken, in a pit in the field and also kept safe from the frost.

In recent years it has been said that brackens are deadly poisonous, but I do not think we old people would agree, as brackens were very widely used in many ways in those far gone days with no ill effects to man or beast.

Mother would always have difficulty getting us in and washed for bed, as when not working we would be playing games with our neighbours until it was quite dark. We all loved the dry, keen frosty weather, it being one of our favourite times, as we had such good places for sliding and sledging. We used to work ourselves up until we felt really roasted and had to shed some of our warm clothes.

Each season gave us different pastimes when we were not working. My eldest brother and his pal loved it when our horse, like ourselves, was free. She was such a good-natured pet that she would come running to them when they called her. All our animals knew their names, and often in the summer we would be sent to fetch home the cows for milking as they had a habit of wandering pretty far away while eating. Yet they would come when called, as they knew it was milking time.

Meg, our horse, seemed to be in her glory with the boys, when they would take her to a dyke or fence so as to get on her back, even without any tackle and them even on their bare feet. She would trot happily about with them, while they held on by her mane. Yes, it was a lovely life, always sharing with the animals.

The chickens also gave us much delight, as sometimes mother would be lamenting a hen having gone missing, when suddenly she would reappear, so proud with a lovely brood of chicks, but herself looking very poor and thin. It certainly was a God-given blessing being brought up in such a lovely part of the country, surrounded by animals and all other small, humble creatures.

Once we were grown up and the grandchildren came on holiday, I relived my childhood all over again, as they too loved sharing with the animals. Mother's little terrier was a great favourite, but once, having had pups, the children must have annoyed her for, to our surprise, the pups suddenly disappeared, and this was before their eyes had opened. So although we watched her movements as often as we could, she took very good care not to go near her hiding place while anyone was about. Then, after a few weeks, she proudly brought home a strong, sturdy litter of playful pups and enjoyed sitting and having the grandchildren play with them. She even brought home a young rabbit, dead of course, and dropped it among the pups to play with and, likely as not, to train them.

Going back to our own childhood, we would always get up

as early as we could, hoping mother would still be out at the milking. My brother would then help me to get ready for school, thinking we were helping mother, as she was always so busy. Alas, we often caused her extra work, such as the time we polished our boots with blacklead, the grate polish – what a dirty mess! Then, instead of Vim for cleaning as in later years, it was a square cake-like soap called Monkey Brand, with the picture of a monkey. My brother took this to wash my face, and said it would get rid of all the sun freckles that my face seemed to be covered with, but, oh my, it also got rid of the skin and caused me plenty of pain.

Always, before the break-up for the school summer holidays, the Laird would pay a visit to the school to find out about the scholars who would be leaving. When my turn came, the secretary from the mansion house called on mother to say that Mrs. Craig Sellar, the lady of the mansion, would like me to take up work in the mansion as the fifth housemaid when our summer holiday was over. Fifth housemaid meant that I would be a maid for the staff only, my way of being trained for attending on the gents later on.

I never saw the film *Upstairs, Downstairs*, but I am told it reflected life for my generation. One thing I can honestly say is that we were treated very well in every way.

The mansion was a beautiful house all through, and very modern for the time, as it had only recently been built. The reason for this was that two estates, bordering each other, were united through marriage. The staff quarters were most comfortable, being richly carpeted and curtained and with good quality furniture. Of course, the estate owners were millionaires and the place as a whole was a show-piece, kept in perfect order.

Discipline was very strict and anyone wishing to be out after 10 p.m. had to have special permission. Meal hours had also to be strictly adhered to, especially the lunch which was at 1 o'clock, as the gents' lunch came after at 1.30. With the exception of the kitchen staff, all the others had lunch together at a large table in the servants' hall. At ten minutes to one a small bell rang on the upstairs landing, this signalled that all women must stop work immediately, go to our bedrooms and get smartened up, then make for the top landing where we all waited for a second bell. From highest to lowest we all then tripped downstairs, first being the ladies' maids, then the housemaids, myself being at the tail end. As we reached the main floor there, as were the woman upstairs, all the men lined up outside the dining hall from highest to lowest. They started with the valets, butlers, footmen, hallboy, and oddman, like myself, bringing up the rear.

We women passed by on to our places at the table without taking the slightest notice of the men as we entered the hall, they then followed us in turn to their respective places at the table, the butler's place always being at the top of the table where he did the carving. He would pass the plates on to the first footman, who sat next to him as each portion was carved and he, in turn, would serve a vegetable onto the plates. The plates would then be passed on to the second footman for another vegetable, then to the hall boy, who dished out potatoes, and so on until all were served. Each person helped themselves to gravy from the boats on the table.

We generally had a three-course lunch which was really splendid, the best of everything, same as was served to the gents. Little talk was indulged in as time was short, the men having to serve the gents' lunch immediately after. So it was, at the end of the meal the butler said the Grace, after which we would all file out quietly, in order, as we had entered.

The under staff were never allowed to talk unless spoken to, and the lunch time was real agony for us young girls who were also being taught good and proper manners – "etiquette." The footmen, who were well trained and knew the ropes, as it were, loved to torment us young ones by playing tricks to make us laugh, as nerves did cause us to laugh, this being considered rude when no-one knew the cause but ourselves. When dishing out vegetables we'd sometimes get a double helping and at other times very little, such as should it be broad beans or peas, we would get only one on our plate.

The hall boy was just as bad, as when setting the table, he would mix up our cutlery, putting a small sweet spoon for soup and a large soup spoon for the sweet. So, trying to behave like young ladies and ignore all the tricks, really kept us from enjoying a most delicious meal. We would be afraid that trying to suppress our laughter would cause us to cough, or worse, to choke.

For other meals the heads dined on their own, their room being known as the stewards' room, them having more time to relax as the gents for those meals were served first. The rest of the staff all dined together in the servants' hall, but at a smaller table, and we were served there by the first footman, who sat at the top of the table. As we, too, had more time to relax, we did enjoy those meals, no tricks were played and all talked freely. For supper we always got two courses, meat and vegetables, etc. and a sweet. Later, about 9 o'clock, we helped ourselves from a tea tray with light snacks such as biscuits or cake.

While referring to the kindness of the estate gents, this has brought more recollections of schooldays to mind.

On closing day, before the start of the Christmas holidays, we all had to come to school dressed in our Sunday best as we were leaving, after lunch, to go down to the mansion house for our Christmas tree party. This caused great excitement as no work was done, the teacher lecturing us on good manners, so as to be on our best behaviour.

The village school children also being present, she always wanted we, her children, to outshine them. Hence, before leaving, she would bring in a face cloth and towel and saw to it that we were nice and clean and our hair nicely brushed. The cart then arrived, nicely decorated, the only conveyance, as I have already stated, in those long gone days. Even the ordinary cycles were not to be had until some years later.

Last date of entry was June 24th 1993.

Today is the 5th February, 1994, and I open this jotter once more for future entries to please my good friends and my young nephews and nieces. I have tried a few times to make a fresh start but it was hopeless, I just had to close the jotter and put it away. So it's a pleasant surprise that I am in the mood this morning, for I was seeing myself becoming less able with age. However, if it's the good Lord's will that I keep writing I will.

Early this week, about 5 p.m., I had just locked my door and started to prepare my supper of fish and toast, when someone came knocking at the door. So, unlocking and opening the door, I had a very pleasant surprise. There was a niece's husband with two beautiful, feathered, cock pheasants. He had been out shooting with his boss on his country estate. What did please me so much was that he put himself over 30 miles off his journey home to deliver such a lovely gift to his old aunt.

The estate, here in Argyll, was known as Oramsary, and from here in the town of Oban to his home in Bishopton, Renfrewshire – I do not know the mileage – is a steady drive of between 2½ to 3 hours. Whereas going directly home via Lochgilphead near Oramsary, would have been much shorter.

I always feel very touched and humbled by the many kindnesses shown me in so many different and unexpected ways, that I know for certain that God does work his miracles through chosen people. If He did not, I would never have met such wonderful people through such wonderful and strange circumstance. I have also learned that He, at times, turns the wrath of man to His glory.

Now I shall return to the 24th June 1993. It turned out to be a lovely sunny day in the midst of very changeable weather, cold and wet, for summer. So I said to myself: First thing in the morning, Agnes, this is your birthday come round once more, so count your many blessings and prepare to spend it quietly on your own, remembering your great age. Think on past memories, when things were so different and now most all the family and old friends enjoying their "Eternal Rest", and whom I so often think are still with us in spirit, as the good book, The Bible, says, we are surrounded by a Heavenly host of witnesses. "A happy thought."

As I have said previously, I am no scholar, but very satisfied with my humble lot, the good book being my constant help and companion, having an answer to my many problems which at time seem very strange. "A wonderful encyclopaedia."

On clearing-up and finishing my usual morning jobs after my breakfast of porridge, tea, toast and marmalade, I sat down to spend the forenoon writing until my simple lunch of steamed haddock, done on a buttered plate on top of the pan where I cook a couple of potatoes and a few vegetables, frozen, or whatever is in season. Yes, I've learned for the past few years to take the easiest way with everything as my energy gets less, and daily count my blessings that I can do so very much myself, and keep my home clean and respectable.

I was getting on nicely with my writing but, before it was time to put on my simply-made lunch, in the quietness I heard someone walk in the front door. Oh, what a lovely surprise! Here was my niece and her husband from Bishopston on a surprise visit to spend my birthday with me, and in time to take me out for lunch. It didn't take me long to close my jotter and get ready, after checking on my birthday gifts – my favourite, two pheasants out of the deep-freeze, a section of honey and a box of chocolates.

My nephew buys a lot of the cock pheasants, as they are generally sold at the shoot, and come in most useful these days when food, I don't think, is as tasty as when I was young. All I enjoy now is pheasant and venison, though sadly, we do not get much venison these days as I understand that most of it goes abroad, especially to Germany.

After lunch, we went up to the hospital to see my brother, who was there getting a leg ulcer seen to. We then went on to view a very nice "Eventide Home" that I was deciding that I should move in to, however, I am still here.

Feb. 9th.: Suddenly had to lay down the pen to relax the old hand and eyes. I thought that unless I can spend more time writing, the book, if it ever gets finished will be like "Burns' Scotch Haggis" – all mixed up and repeats. That is, unless the good Lord answers my prayers to keep my brain fairly clear so as the old stories that my friends and young relations long so much to learn about, can be told. There is also the unhappy thought that I may be forgetting the most interesting.

Back in my young days as a housemaid to the staff in the castle on the Ardtornish estate, where we had our home for over forty-nine years, I seemed to turn from a schoolgirl to a grown-up in a day as I had to pin up my pleats and change my school dress for one down to my ankles. Little chance of getting a university education in those far gone days, plenty of hard honest work being the order of the day. Never did we hear such evil as seems an everyday occurrence now.

My first job in the morning was to clean out the housemaids' sitting room fireplace and set the fire. This I did not enjoy doing as there was so much brass to be kept nicely polished such as the fender, tongs, etc. Of course I had a large dust sheet spread on the carpet before starting work so there was never a mess left, and we also got clean dust sheets weekly. I'd then have a good wash, after which it was time to go and call Mrs. Craig Sellar's lady's maid, with a can of hot water.

Mrs. Sellar was the estate owner, a beautiful stately lady in appearance, and good and kind as well as beautiful. I think her age at this time would have been over ninety years old as I was only in my teens when she died. She visited her people fairly often, and I remember, when I was quite young, her saying to mother, as she stood at the gate, looking round, when leaving: "I do envy you in your small cottages."

Our home couldn't be called a cottage but, of course, it was very small compared to the castle, it being built as a shooting lodge. Sometimes such houses were used as dowager houses.

After breakfast, when all the ladies and gents were called, it was back upstairs to work. Each of us had to get our premises spic and span with a place for everything and everything must be in its place. The sweeping of floors was done by getting down on one's knees with a stiff-bristled hand brush and pan. Fortunately, the carpets were all of the best, and so thick as to cause no hurt to our knees.

Bedrooms had to be slopped twice daily from a wash stand, where all washed in those days, whatever their station in life. There was a nice set of china comprising, a large cold water jug sitting in a large wash basin, water carafe and tumbler resting on top, tooth dishes and brushes and, of course, the soap dish. There were lovely designs on the china, and all of good quality, so the wash stand looked very nice. Of course, the hot water cans had to be collected and taken back to the working pantry. Each of the staff, when going to wash, collected their own, I had only to return them when doing the bedrooms.

Me being the 5th housemaid, and as I said, the tail-end and lowest, I was always working in staff quarters which was very lonely. I got the 4th housemaid to help me with the beds, which I enjoyed. Of course, the head came at odd times to check on me, but I did not look forward to her visits, for although I did my best, I was always afraid it would not please her as she was most particular.

In the evenings when the butler and footmen were serving dinner, the housemaids would be in the bedrooms tidying up and putting away all the clothes that were lying about, doing down beds, cleaning up the fireplaces and stoking the fire so that the rooms would be nice and warm for when people retired for bed. At the same time, I would be doing the same thing in the staff rooms.

This was my way of being trained, but coming from a strict home, where we children were well trained and had to obey orders, also to use our common sense, I really was not interested in continuing with such work. So mother had to explain for me, as we as the unders, were never allowed to speak unless spoken to.

So I got my wish, and to say I was happy was an understatement. I was in my glory and in an entirely different world in every way − this being in the kitchen. As there was the complete staff of five, I was taken on as an extra. The kitchen was a lovely place to work in, being very large, and the walls such a brilliant shining white − I've never seen anything like it since. The shelves all around the walls were a brilliant sight, with all shapes and sizes of pans, for all kinds of cooking, also all kind of moulds. Everything had to be, not enough to say shining, they had to glitter. If this was not the case, when the chef came in to start cooking dinner he passed no remark, only walked along, picking anything that was tarnished and dropping them into the pan sink in the scullery. The only other thing on the wall was a large, nice clock. Like upstairs, in the house-maids' department, there was a place for everything and every-thing had to be put in its place.

This pleased me for nature blessed me with a tidy mind, and I would never fall asleep if I went to bed, even when tired, and leave my clothes untidy where I dropped them off. I would end up getting out of bed and putting things in order after which I would soon fall asleep.

My goings-on often annoyed my parents, but in later years, during the war, I was rushed by lifeboat to hospital in Oban because of stomach ulcers. Hence the reason, when I was called up for service, the doctor said I could go home as I would only be a liability.

Back to the kitchen. The other most interesting thing was the table, it was so large it had to be taken into the kitchen in sections. It was not out of the usual for breadth, but length, as it had six thick legs and the table top itself must have been several inches thick. Instead of drawers on both sides, each drawer could be pulled open from either side. In each drawer sections kept all sorts of knives and tools separate. As there were three large drawers in the table, and with so many tools, it took me time to know what each was for. Of course, with the size and weight of the table, it could never be moved.

We had very long hours in the kitchen, but being interesting and enjoyable work, we were all happy, and I was allowed to talk freely like the rest. Of course, all the staff were well trained and superior, or they weren't in Ardtornish. The chef was a thorough gent, as were the butler and valet. Never once did I see the chef angry, and he talked so gently, but he did get a bit excited when there were large house parties and special func-tions on.

There was *never* any smoking in the castle, nor did I ever see anyone the worse for drink, such things were unheard of.

Although I never worked with another chef, I chanced to see a few in recent years when visiting restaurants, and was anything but impressed. Our chef was always immaculate, with a good quality short white jacket and white apron. This he always changed twice daily, the second time when he came in to start dinner. Likewise his light fawn trousers and shoes were of the same good quality. He also wore a nice, smart white hat, and with such a lovely corn coloured thick wave of hair up the front, and with his nearly always smiling face, he made a very handsome picture. He never checked his staff, but always explained things nicely.

To start with, my work as an extra was to help with all kinds of jobs, such as putting various ingredients through different sized strainers, using a wooden oval-shaped thing with a catch at the back the size of a saucer. What this implement was called, I forget. The first thing I did was to learn what all the knives and tools were for. This I had to do by checking the menu books daily, when I would be shown by one of the girls what things would be required for use when preparing each course, in order. Then I had to lay out, also in order, all the things the chef would require to use, at his special side part of the table, as no-one worked from either end.

Most times I worked beside the chef, and that was most interesting. On Saturdays we had extra work, making aspic jelly and lots of other things, in preparation for doing cold meals on Sundays for the dining room. We would have whole salmons coated with aspic, and done up as if alive, on prepared beds of salad, and all on silver dishes. The fancy dishes were endless, no scarcity of anything for cooking, and it was a lot of hard work getting all the fancy dishes done, even if so interesting.

How different since the war years. One doesn't get such variety or nearly such lovely tasting food of any kind. Of course, most is now bought ready-made in packets.

I often wonder what the ingredients are. For instance, meringues are now made from seaweed, no such thing as egg whites, and aspic jelly is from packets – both only requiring added water. We made our aspic jelly by first making a clear soup by boiling very slowly best fresh hough, having added different herbs, no vegetables, then straining through a special fine soup cloth, then returned to a well-washed soup pan. A dozen fresh eggs were carefully washed and separated, with the whites being beaten until very stiff, and all the eggshells were crushed. The shells were then dropped into the soup pan, followed by the well-beaten whites. The pan had not to be moved more than necessary, but watched carefully until it just came slowly to boiling point for one minute. Once again it was strained through a soup cloth, and on Sunday, we had lovely, tasty, clear aspic jelly, while all the whites came onto the soup cloths just as it was dropped onto the soup like the crushed shells, so gelatine was used to stiffen. That just gives an idea of the hard work done in the old days for all kinds of cooking, nothing came easily.

Two other things I dreaded, as they made my young arms ache. Standing at the large, hot range beating eggs and sugar in a large bowl over a pan of hot water for sponge cakes and sweets. Apart from a painful arm, I felt almost cooked myself with the heat of the range. It must be remembered that there was no other way to cook then, but on the coal-fired range.

At least doing the mayonnaise was free from the hot range. I took a large size bottle of olive oil and cut a nick out of the cork, so that only a drip at a time dropped into a bowl, into which I had first put a salt spoonful of dry mustard mix with a little white vinegar. Then I started stirring with a wooden spoon, while holding with my left hand the olive oil bottle upside down for the oil to drip slowly. This could not be hurried, otherwise the mayonnaise would not thicken. Very occasionally, I required to stop the olive oil and drop in a little vinegar, being most careful not to overdo this. I cannot remember exactly how long this took, but I felt exhausted and both arms ached by the time the last drop left the olive oil bottle.

How many months I worked in the kitchen, I cannot remember, but when the staff left for the London house after the New Year pheasant shoot, I joined them to be vegetable and scullery maid. Scullery maid meant that I had to wash all the dishes and pans used in the kitchen, but the main thing was the vegetables. This took a year learning the many kinds of vegetables and all the many ways of preparing and cooking them, to go with the different meats and game dishes.

Of course, I also had to learn to pluck, clean and truss all kinds of game birds, and also learn the proper cuts and joints of meat. I learned this early, being an extra one in the kitchen. The chef was really kind, he always stood at the game sink plucking with me, and I remember that I always thought the bird he started was easier done than mine, so we exchanged them, with him smiling.

One thing I was so pleased and very proud about was when the chef took a bad cold one weekend, and was off duty when there were several guests staying. This worried him, so we in the kitchen decided we would work doubly hard for his sake. We knew he would get all the information from the butler regarding the meals going into the dining room. The chef's cold cured me of my dislike of plucking and preparing smelly birds, for I was determined, like the others, not to let him down. I prepared nineteen game birds that weekend, some of course very small, which were always cooked for breakfast. I can only remember the name of snipes which were for breakfast.

The oddman had an early morning start to stoke the boiler furnace for hot water and another furnace for the central heating, but first he cleaned out and stoked the huge kitchen range, then, before shovelling on the coal, he boiled the kettle on the sticks and made a pot of tea, which he returned to enjoy once he had opened up the flues of the furnaces. By this time the footmen had joined him, and then when the news got round of morning tea, we housemaids also tripped downstairs for a cup – I then being a housemaid. So by the time poor John, the oddman, returned to the kitchen the teapot was empty, and all of the culprits had vanished. After this, there was no teapot to be seen, so John had the kitchen, and a full teapot, to himself in peace. Teaching us a lesson, he had put the teapot in the oven.

Another of John's jobs was to take the brock down each day for the farm pigs. On seeing all the good food being put out, he decided to keep a pig also, although it was only people with ground and animals who did. So John, with the pig in his shed, caused some amusement, but he got the last laugh as his pig weighed in the heaviest of all on the estate, ours included, and he got the brock honestly from the chef.

He never enjoyed his lunch with the crowd in the hall. He loved coming into the kitchen, whenever he could think up an excuse, so the chef, as a favour, allowed him to take his lunch in the kitchen on his own at a small side table, while we were kept busy preparing the dining room lunch. At the same time the different courses had to go into the servants hall, and if we failed to notice he was ready for his second course, he soon sounded his gong by way of an imitation cough. He really had his funny ways, but was always kind and obliging.

The year was spent between Ardtornish and London, going down to London mid-January, and back mid-June. In the London house, in Princes Gate, where we were next door to the American Ambassador, life was fairly quiet. There were no large parties, just more or less old friends and relations, like Mrs.

C. Sellar, who visited, and at times stayed for company, as her son was often from home with his valet. Mrs. Sellar's friends, being old like herself, the meals were very simple and of few courses.

On going back to Ardtornish, life there made up for the quietness of Princes Gate. To begin with, in June there was the fishing, in autumn, the stag shoots, followed by the hinds and, lastly, the pheasant shoots starting in November, when we had the largest house parties. Some of the gents brought their own keepers while, of course, the ladies always brought their personal maids. When the gents brought their keepers, the keepers replaced their valets, so Mr. Gerard C. Sellar's valet did for them.

Pheasants were always reared on the estate. Two pheasant men were kept, only seeing to pheasants, apart from the gamekeepers. Hence, when there were large shooting parties, lunches were sent out daily. A large urn of Irish stew was made for the beaters, these being all the young men on the estate. Their second course was large, delicious, soft biscuits flavoured with caraway seed and cheese, with soft drinks and beer. The biscuits were a great favourite with everyone, and bought regularly by householders from their grocers. I remember they were changed for another kind, which were definitely not nearly so nice, and the demand for them dropped. Sadly, that ended the caraway biscuits, which were a good meal in themselves, being the size of a saucer. The gents' lunch was also sent out, that being pretty much as they would have had indoors.

Being the under housemaid for the staff, I should have travelled down to London the previous year, but mother would not allow me, being too young at fifteen years. I had to stay at Ardtornish with the other housemaids, and the fourth housemaid travelled to London instead to keep the staff quarters. The housemaids, with the exception of the under, never travelled, as they had the whole of the castle to spring-clean. That took six months, working very hard from 8 a.m. until 5 p.m. all week, except Sunday. The head was a terror for perfection, which caused her to be hard on me as she really did not want me, being so young. I would not have stayed myself, if I could have left, but belonging to the estate, Mrs. C. Sellar wanted to keep me, so the head had no option but to put up with me.

I always got up at 7 o'clock and did out our sitting room, then washed and went down to the kitchen to set the breakfast for 8 o'clock, while the second cooked it, and woe betide us if we were late. Our meals were taken in the kitchen for handiness, except for night snacks which were taken to the sitting room on a tray. I had to keep the kitchen and all its premises clean, such as the scullery, several larders, china cupboard and servants hall. The kitchen table had to be scrubbed white each Saturday, which was almost a day's work in itself, and I had also to scrub under the edge all the way round.

I did everything I was told, faithfully giving of my best, but one day, while doing under the ledge, a loose skelf sliced my thumbnail off. I fainted with the pain and was quite ill, my whole arm ached and my hand was useless. Instead of sympathy from the head, she said that I did it to escape work. I though that a cruel thing to say when I always took an interest in my work, and probably did it as well as the fourth would, even if she was much older. This being my second year in Ardtornish Castle, I was sixteen at the time of the accident and very slim, so could have looked younger, which likely turned her against me.

Apart from John, the oddman, working with us during the six months, we had several of the estate workers also, such as the clerk of works. He wound all the clocks each week, and also cleaned the beautiful chandeliers, which were then slipped into special white cotton bags, like pillow slips, with drawing tapes to seal them. Each bag was marked for room and special size, which made the task of fitting so many very simple, even if the cleaning was a very particular and sometimes difficult job.

Now I have discovered, as it's just come back to memory, it was my first year, when fifteen years old, that I replaced the fourth housemaid to stay on at Ardtornish for cleaning. When the staff and household returned in June, I stayed on in the kitchen to start as one of the kitchen staff, namely, "Vegetable Scullerymaid," as my wonderful title.

Once all were back in June, the housemaids in Princes Gate, started their cleaning of the house.

It was the following January that I first went down to London, and having so much less work to do in Princes Gate, we had lots of time off. I enjoyed London, being out at every chance, making up for our busy times at Ardtornish, where at least we, the kitchen staff, had very little free time.

We made lots of new friends by going to Pont Street Church each Sunday, where there was an enjoyable meeting to begin with in the church hall that ended with tea, before going into the church for the evening service. Nearly all the people we made friends with were like ourselves, the staff from mansion houses, and policemen, for employment was scarce up in Scotland at the time, especially in the Highlands. There was no chance of being able to afford a university education, as nothing in those far gone days was free, and wages a mere pittance.

I remember how tall, well-built, and handsome all the police on the street were. Of course, they had to be of a certain height and also fairly well educated, as there were plenty of men to pick from.

In later years when I visited London, I noticed a big difference in the police – they seemed much smaller men and there were also so many in cars on the streets.

What life in London is like today, 1994, I do not know, and

have no desire to find out, as in visiting Glasgow and Edinburgh, as they are anything but the lovely, clean cities of the past. The reason is that life has changed from the days of cheap labour and, as the saying goes, the pendulum has now swung too far in the opposite direction.

Another place we liked visiting was the Wembley Exhibition which, fortunately, was on when I was down there. We liked nosing into every corner until our purses emptied, and that sure did not take long! How we did it was that one did the paying, instead of each paying separately, and when her purse emptied, the other paid. How different from today, we never checked on what each spent, nor referred to it, as our pay was pretty much the same. We just kept enough to take us back to Princes Gate.

Once, on coming out of Pont Street Church, when the sermon, service, prayer, and singing had been especially good, we gave most of what we had in our purses, and decided that we would walk back, taking a longer way. Alas, we got lost and so had to ask our way, and we got much kindness shown us by being taken and put on a bus, with our fare paid, and the driver told where we were to get off.

The bobby we asked was Scottish and I remember him saying; "If I was off duty, I'd take you home myself." Now, we had wandered a long way out of the busy thoroughfare and there were very few police to be seen, but the driver of the bus made sure we would be all right by putting us in the care of another. Eventually, we got back safely, after two hours wandering – a lesson we never forgot.

I was often sending home for a little money, fortunately mother had cash of her own that helped to bring us up, as father's pay as a shepherd, honestly did not feed us. Of course, he had several benefits beside, such as a lovely home, plenty of ground, and good quality houses in the steadings for all the animals. He built a special house for our pig, away on its own in a lovely spot, taking in part of our garden. Our pig had a lovely clean and contented life, able to go in and out and enjoy the sunshine as she wished. In the end, we got beautiful, firm, sweet bacon, what one never can now, the way pigs are fed and kept in large piggeries.

It must be made clear that it was not the Laird or his mother who were responsible for the poor wages, as they had men in all different departments on the estate to see to different things. Anyone who saw the estate could see how beautiful everything was and kept in perfect condition. There were two men painting full time all the year round, likewise, two joiners, a blacksmith and others besides. This had to be so as the Laird took in everything that nothing dared to be neglected.

I remember two families I met had servants of their own, they being, of course, head servants, and I often heard our parents, and others, say that the Sellars would have been horrified had they known how small the wages were, as they, themselves, were especially kind, always visiting and giving expensive gifts.

Even we children in school were given toothbrushes, that giving an idea how very caring they were. At our Christmas Tree party, every child was given a lovely, good-quality, scarlet jersey along with a suitable gift and a bag full of fruit, sweets and cakes. I can only remember my first gift of a beautiful doll with golden hair. Her large blue eyes, with lovely eyelashes, would close when laid down, and I could see her teeth, as she at times made a crying sound. I was so excited, and yet everything is so very vivid to me when talking of the past.

Mother had a trying time with her brood of four when we returned home laden, as the excitement and noise was such that we didn't want to go to bed. Thinking back, my doll must have been very expensive as she was china, beautifully dressed and with real, wee shoes. Sadly, she came to grief as my young brother dropped her on the cement pavement, which was round the house. Children of today get so much, that they don't experience the joy we got from the very few gifts we received then.

The Ardtornish Estate, at that time, was supposed to be the best in Argyll. Today, I think it would be honest to say it's the very reverse, as it has deteriorated so much in every way. Worse, I felt when visiting, were all the lovely rivers with banks eaten into and large, solid, concrete-pillared bridges, that should last for years, lying in the river, leaving no way for some lovely walks, or to get to the lovely fishing lochs and boathouse and its good boats. The boathouse going the same way as the bridges, and so much more.

Back to mind. Mrs. Sellar also supplied both schools on the estate with smashing good cocoa for the children to have at lunchtime with our peaces. This kind of cocoa I've never seen since I left school, and it was never sold in any shops at the time. It was in a sealed tin, being like Nestles condensed milk, a thick paste, and tasted lovely, just like chocolate if eaten out of the tin. We children used to eat most of ours out of our cups before the teacher reached us with her kettle of boiling water.

Now, to my great shame, I will clear my conscience, and say that my small girlfriend and I took a tin out of the school. How we did it, I cannot remember, and how we were able to open it, I've no recollection either, unless it was opened when we took it. One thing I do remember, when talking of schooldays since, is the wrong we did in stealing.

So young children, even coming out of good homes, can have an evil streak in them. We knew full well we had done wrong, and found an ideal place in which to hide the tin – in our pig house. At this time, the poor pig was part of our breakfast, so the tin was safe from prying eyes. The place was spotlessly clean, as father was most particular in all his work, keeping the inner part of the sleeping quarters with plenty of nice dry hay, so the tin was well, and safely, put out of sight.

I remember all our pigs were clean animals also, as they kept their house so clean, using the outer parts of the corners of their large outhouse as their toilet. If the pig was resting when we went down to feed her, she was all covered in hay and lying just inside the entrance, all we could see was her snout. She must have been listening, for she only went inside, out of sight, at night, and each pig acted the same. I dreaded being sent to feed her as her hearing was so good, and if she was hungry, before I got to the stye to pour her food into the trough, she would be jumping up to get into the bucket. It was no fun getting the food poured into the trough, without smacking her with a switch, which I didn't like to do. I used to walk as quietly as I could, when nearing the stye, but in spite of all this, she heard me as I had to pass through the beautiful avenue, and when the leaves had fallen in the autumn, the swish of my going through leaves, just could not be done silently.

Father washed and scrubbed the pig once a week in real buttermilk, and she simply loved that, grunting with pleasure all the time, and it left her hair looking silvery shining on her pure white skin. Also, being well fed with plenty of milk and porridge, potatoes and vegetables, meant that we had good crackling besides the very tasty bacon.

Which reminds me. My late sister once spent a few days with her in-laws on their farm in Newton Mearns, and when she was leaving, they gave her a roasting gigot of pork. It really turned her when she saw and compared their large piggery with our small, clean one. How she grudged taking it home all the long journey to Tobermory in Mull. To her delight, our visitor was in – our minister – so she gladly presented him with a gift of roast pork, which he gratefully accepted. I know, for I was there, as I always went from home to help keep house for her two small boys, when she was away from home.

It has just come to mind, that the cocoa got in school must have come from the Army and Navy Stores in London, as it was from there that all the Ardtornish stores came from, hence, why it was not to be had elsewhere.

On returning to Ardtornish in June, when I then started properly with the kitchen staff, my working abode was the scullery, with my title, "vegetable maid". I was supposed to take a year to learn all about the different vegetables, ways of preparing and cooking, and which to be served with different meats and game dishes. I also had to learn, in the year, all about the various game birds – plucking, cleaning and preparing. This I had learned, with the help of the chef, the season before when I was taken on as an extra hand in the kitchen, having wanted to leave the housework, so this was a big advantage for me. There was also the fish, salmon and trout, which I had to clean and prepare, apart from washing and cleaning all dishes and tools, pots and pans, all copper, and roasting tins, etc.

It was constant work, but working in good, happy conditions and company, I did not mind the long hours of hard work. We had to be out of the kitchen by 3 o'clock, and restart at 6 o'clock. I seldom stopped, until the chef was told, and he would come and chase me out. I wanted to see all my brass taps shining, hence my working late. There were ten of them and they were not small taps, but large like the sinks. There were five sinks, two for washing up dishes and pans, with one in between with plain hot water for dropping dishes into when washed, pans were also dropped into this when washed. There was also one for game and one for fish.

All pots and pans, being copper, had to be cleaned with a mixture of silver sand and flour mixed with vinegar, and unless they were put into very hot clean water from the washing sink, and then thoroughly dried, they quickly tarnished. I determined that once I took over the work, the chef would never get the chance to take any off the kitchen shelves, as he did on starting at 6 p.m., if tarnished, when I worked with him as extra hand.

I was really happy any time I chanced to see the head house-maid, knowing that she was not now my boss. Sadly, however, she decided soon after to leave, but it was quite evident that she was not a well person, neither was she young. Today, I feel sure that her illness would be diagnosed as Dementia. She did not intend to retire, only have the summer resting. With her splendid reference from Ardtornish, she was offered a post with Royalty, but said she was in a large enough Royalty and wished a much smaller and more relaxing place.

Once again, at the end of the season, before moving to London, Mrs. C. Sellar's personal friend and assistant visited mother to say I was now quite able to move as 2nd into the kitchen, but being so young, decided it best I should go elsewhere for a year and get other ideas, and return to Ardtornish as 1st. So I was given the choice between Hopetown House with the Marchioness of Linlithgow, or Lady Stuart Clarke of Dundas. For some reason I cannot remember, I went with Lady Stuart Clarke at Dundas Castle.

I do not recollect much of Dundas except for Tennis Week, when the fleet was anchored in Port Edgar. Each day for the week, officers of a different ship came up to play against a different house party at Dundas, with the ships' officers bringing with them their ship's band.

It was a very busy time for us in the kitchen as all came in for lunch, including the ships' bands. We did not have a chef, but a quite capable cook. Unfortunately she took ill, and was taken to hospital shortly before Tennis Week and, being the height of the season, it was impossible to get the right person. The cook who came meant that I had to shoulder the responsibility, which was rather much for me. However, our busy week soon ended, and we could not have done too badly, as a gift of cash was sent down for all the kitchen staff from the officers, and we were congratulated on the lunches sent up. How much money was sent down we never heard, as cook did not say.

We had masses of fruit in the garden, so each day we made plenty of strawberry and raspberry ice cream by pulping the fruit and mixing only with our own lovely, rich, farm cream which had been whipped. It was the best ice cream I have ever tasted, but the most difficult to make, as the freezer was a contraption of a box with a handle which was to be constantly turned until our mixture froze evenly. The ice cream container was fixed into the centre of the box, then round it was placed a layer of coarse salt and a layer of chopped ice, layer upon layer until the box was filled. Then came the horrible task of turning the handle, which we all had to do in turns.

One thing I did not have to worry about was, with their being a different party each day, I did not have the bother of changing the menu and I always got the cook to decided on the easiest courses. Had I not had my good grounding as an extra hand in the Ardtornish kitchen, I dread to think how we would have done.

Within a year of my leaving Ardtornish, good, kind, old Mrs. Sellar's health started failing, as did her memory. Therefore, they returned early to Princes Gate where, in London, Mrs. Sellar would have the best of care. Mr. Sellar only returned to

Ardtornish for short spells to fish and to shoot, with a skeleton staff in the kitchen and butler's pantry. It was an understood thing how devoted he was to his mother, and supposedly his reason for not marrying. It was also known that he was not too strong, having heart trouble.

The car and chauffeur were left in London for Mrs. Sellar's benefit. Mr. Sellar would then travel up to Ardtornish by train with his valet. Very sadly, on one occasion while returning to London, he as usual in his 1st class compartment, and his valet in 3rd class, only occasionally going to see if he required anything, he was found dead by the ticket collector. He was sitting with his pipe in his hand, having suffered a heart attack, with no chance of help with him being on his own. This happened between Oban and Edinburgh, I cannot remember what station, but the valet, from a corner window seat, watched all the commotion and saw the covered stretcher being carried from the train never realising that it was his own kind boss who had died, until nearing Edinburgh, when he went along to prepare him for leaving the train.

By this time his mother's memory was quite gone, and soon after she, too, passed away, leaving all their employees to mourn their loss. Thankfully, the old lady never knew of her beloved son's passing. Their deaths brought great changes to Ardtornish Estate and all the people. I never returned to the mansion house.

I cannot remember when I left Dundas, but I must have been nineteen years of age, as I think it was the year of the General Strike, 1926, when life was dreadfully hard for us, the working class, with people going hungry. Yet, as I learned in later years, people on the whole were peaceable, law-abiding, honest and well behaved, apart from a few rogues. It meant Dundas taking on a nightwatchman, who came on duty at 8 p.m. and finished at 6 a.m. I remember that his last job, before going off duty, was to call all the staff in the morning, which he did only as a favour to us. He was a nice, friendly, helpful man, who did odd jobs in the castle until 10 p.m., such as helping in the butler's pantry cleaning all the knives. There were no such things as stainless steel knives then, each knife was put into a separate slot in a machine and a handle turned, which both polished and sharpened the knives. Another job I recall he did, was to polish all boots and shoes.

His nightly abode was the butler's pantry, and we in the kitchen sent up a jolly good supper for him, and sandwiches for through the night. He also made tea for himself as he wished. He had to walk round the outside and inside of the castle several times during the night. Happily, no rogues came near the castle to disturb our peace.

On leaving Dundas, it was my turn to stay at home to help with the work, as previously it was my eldest sister who had done this. She then went to the Agricultural College in Kilmarnock, which was her choice, my other sister being in Edinburgh attending the Atholl Crescent, the domestic science college, which was her choice. She never liked working at home because of all the kinds of outdoor jobs. So I took on the responsibility of caring for the home, which I was very happy to be able to do, making mother's life so much more relaxing and restful, after her very, very busy life bringing us all up so healthy, strong and splendid in every way.

As the years rolled past, and my parents no longer young, it gave me an inner glow of happiness and thankfulness to God as we sat round a nice, comfortable fire after our high tea at 5.30 p.m., to listen to the radio, starting with the 6 o'clock news. I always had to make quick work of clearing up so as to get finished in time.

Mother's little terrier lay toasting in front of the fire, at our feet, until the heat got too much for him, when he would then sit on each person's knee, in turn, until that also got too hot

*The Robertson sisters from Morvern.*

*Grandad Robertson, Morvern.*

*Granny Robertson, taken 1948, when shopping in Oban.*

*School group. Three Robertson girls in tartan dresses with teacher.*
*Brother is at front in kilted suit.*

*Our old school and schoolhouse teacher's home.*

*Five Robertson boys, three of whom are now gone.*
*This was the only time they were together at the old home.*

*The old home where we grew up. Adrtornish, Morvern.*

for him. He would then go and stretch full-length on the floor until the clock struck 7 p.m., at which point he would jump up and go to father, pawing and barking at him, while looking at the clock to remind him it was time to go out to feed the cattle. Just for fun father, knowing what he was up to, never moved for a few minutes, to see what would happen, but the terrier would not stop pawing and barking at him. Then the excitement when father did make move, as what the terrier really wanted was to get out into the fields to chase rabbits, etc. Father would only require to give one good whistle when ready to go home, and the terrier would reappear, happy and contented.

A very simple and contented life for us all, and I learned at an early age, that it is what one puts into life that counts, and brings the most happiness, not what one tries to get out of it.

Like mother, my eldest sister, Tina, was a splendid cook in everything she made, also making delicious butter. Even with such a busy life, mother enjoyed entering at the agricultural shows, and always did quite well, but Tina never did as well, she having other interests.

One thing I learned was that training, as I did in the mansion house, and the good grounding and common sense we learned from mother, was far superior to a domestic science training, for my sister Margaret's cooking was inferior to both mother and Tina. The year I was extra hand in Ardtornish kitchen, I recall that in June, at the start of the season, the 1st was domestic science trained, a nice, smart and good-looking girl, but hopeless at her work. This left the chef with no option but to get rid of her. As for Margaret, she could not have had much interest in cooking, as she had the same chance as Tina and I to learn all with mother.

I enjoyed a contented life at home, knowing I was much

needed, and often having the usual country activities. In the late summer evenings, which were very enjoyable also, we would sometimes cycle 5 miles down to Lochaline, our village, where we would join friends to go fishing on Lochaline, returning home starving, and laden with fish, at about 1 o'clock in the morning. We would then start up the fire with sticks and cook plenty of the fish. These were difficult to clean, being very slippery because of their freshness. After a jolly good, enjoyable, feed, and feeling the benefit of the sea breezes coming in the loch from the Sound of Mull, I was scarcely in bed before I was sound asleep.

In the winter months, we would have dancing and whist drives, it being very amusing as I often got the lowest score, which never troubled me in the least. Whether I was a bad player, or just unlucky with cards, I always did enjoy a game of cards. Only my brother did not like seeing me rise and accept the booby prize, so any time there was a whist drive on he would ask me if I intended going. What he really meant was that I should stay at home but, I would teasingly tell him that the booby prize was better than none. Any time I had a certain man as my partner, and we were playing against his wife, he would play to lose, no matter how good our hands were, therefore getting his wife's side to win. Whether he did the same with the others he played with, I never discussed with anyone, and so never knew, cheating being such a despicable thing, especially in middle-aged men.

February 26th: Alistair, the brother I have just referred to, worked as a steward at sea, returning home in later years to help father, now in old age, with the animals. Now old himself, being 82 years of age, yesterday, the 25th, sadly he had to have his left leg amputated in the local hospital, the result of a very nasty ankle ulcer. He had suffered quite some time, although the doctors did everything possible to heal it. Yesterday, being a lovely day, if cold, I was able to give thanks to the good Lord for his many blessings to me as I enjoyed a lovely, quiet walk over the hill, being a short-cut to the hospital. I was able to spend 1 hour and 20 minutes with him before his operation. I was happy to see him relaxed and looking much better than I had expected, having committed himself to God's will.

Now with his operation, a success, behind him he is resting quietly, and is thankful and contentedly happy, hopeful that he can now look forward to enjoying a lovely spring and summer, having the cold month of March in hospital to recover.

As the years rolled by and neighbours' children, like ourselves, left school and worked on the estate or away elsewhere, we, five of us at the time, all worked on the estate in different departments. This meant that the cutting of peats had to stop, as there was no-one to work the many turns, and the building into little stooks, required to dry them. In reality peats, when cut, were only soft lumps, like mud paste, requiring endless work to turn them into lightweight peats. Working them was quite sore on our hands, as the wind and air caused the paste to dry on them. Still, we children were hardy in those days and knew the work had to be done, so we never grumbled, probably because we knew it would not do us any good, and speaking back to our parents, as some do today, would not be tolerated.

Changing from peat to coal; the coal was delivered to all on the estate, coming by small, hardy boats, known as puffers. These tied up at a small jetty in Lochaline village and emptied into carts from the estate. A crane would take up from the hold of the boat, a bucket holding so many hundredweights, the amount each cart could take, and empty direct by tipping into the cart. When the cart moved away, the next cart took its place. Deliveries were a dreadfully slow tedious job, which took several days, as the distances were long to some houses, such as our own, which was 5 miles from Lochaline. This meant a round trip of 10 miles before taking on another load. Of course, the horse had to have a rest, when the cart was emptied, and have a drink and something to eat, as did the driver who got a meal from mother.

Travelling in the Highlands in the long-distant past was a simple matter compared to today's travelling. The reason being that now mostly all have cars, with the exception of old folk like myself. Like coal, which I have just mentioned, goods of all kinds were brought in large cargo boats from the south to all the islands, and to the surrounding mainland. A certain number of passengers could also travel on the ships, if they were going in one's direction. There were a number of berths provided, and the boats travelled at all times of the day and night. Passenger steamers sailing from Oban daily were, in the past, pretty much as they are today in number, although of no comparison in size and type.

I often wonder what even my parents' generation would think if they could return and see all the changes that have taken place.

In my young days our boat, known as the Mull and Morvern steamer, plied the Sound of Mull daily. Leaving Tobermory at 7.45 a.m., it crossed to Drimmin on the mainland where it stopped, and a small rowing boat came out with the mail and passengers, if anyone was going to Oban for the day, or further south. It then went back to a port in Mull, Salen by name, where the pier was quite busy with a few always joining the steamer, along with plenty of mail and all other kinds of goods, even animals if there was a sale on in Oban.

Next stop was again across on the mainland, Lochaline, following the same routine although it was not such a busy pier. It was then back once more, to stop at Craignure, on the Mull side, where a small motor-boat would come out with the usual complement of passengers, mail, etc. Sometimes this could be quite a busy stop, when a larger motor-boat was used, with even an odd animal among the standing passengers.

Most all on the steamer deck would go to the side to watch the goings-on below of the steamer and motor-boat. Once the engines were started up again, we passengers on deck would turn to leave the side of the steamer, and often a gust of wind whipped hats off heads and sent them spinning in the air, never to return, except for the odd one. We would watch them drop on the water to toss about, get filled, and sink out of sight.

Once, on returning from Edinburgh on holiday, with a velour hat I was very proud of, having spent more on it than I should, the same fate happened to me. Turning from the steamer side, it was whipped off my head. I watched it being tossed up and down with the wind, the steamer merrily steaming on its way, leaving my expensive hat behind. It even rested, or I should have said was blown down, just touching the water when, like a miracle, another gust of wind lifted it up and sent it blowing, to land back on deck where it was caught on the crane. It's a story that is hard to believe, but it's honestly, perfectly true. Subsequently, I got several years wear out it.

In those days, both men and women, even quite young, always wore hats, as one was not considered properly dressed if not. Of course, in the past, people did dress nicely and always had special clothes for Sundays.

Apart from the steamers now sailing daily from Oban, certain ones to certain islands are their only lifeline, carrying people, mails, and goods of all kinds, also animals, when sales were on in Oban. Such goings-on have not changed, except for the steamers themselves being entirely different. Today's modern, huge hulks, are so high up in the water, whereas in the past, they were so much lower in the water, long, streamlined and graceful.

Back to our beloved Mull and Morvern steamer, the Lochinvar by name. From Craignure it sailed direct to Oban, where it was due any time between 10.30 and 11.30 a.m., depending on how busy their trip had been. Leaving Oban again at 1.15 p.m. for the return journey, it would stop at all the ports, and arrive back to dock at Tobermory for the night any time between 4.30 and 5.30 p.m. Our beloved Lochinvar was a hardy wee boat, and it took a real stormy day to keep her in port, not like today's modern, huge, monsters.

Only once did everyone grieve for several hours, feeling sure she was gone with everyone on board, the weather having turned so dreadful on her leaving Oban. She disappeared without a trace from the Sound of Mull, with no way of contact in those days. So many were the prayers sent up to the good Lord for her safety. Joyously, next day, in calmer conditions, she was spotted sailing back safely to us up the Sound, having been driven by the strong winds up Loch Lynnhe. She came new on the Mull run in 1907, and remained with us for years. Sadly, I cannot recollect when she was sold and left us to sail on the Thames, after, of course being modernised.

When she started with us, there was no closed in bridge for the Captain, only a surround of strong canvas up to his shoulders, allowing him to view over. It must have been very unpleasant for him being exposed to all kinds of weather, standing such long hours without exercise to keep warm. In later years, a small bridge was built on the Lochinvar, which was a comfort and a blessing to the good Captain.

I cannot recollect how long she sailed as a pleasure boat on the Thames, but once again our dear wee pleasure boat was sold. Strangely, a young Oban man, living down south, saw the sale notice. So with excitement, he decided to buy her, and return her back to the old haunts as a seasonal pleasure steamer. Very sadly things did not turn out as he had hoped. She was in port as he prepared for the return journey by loading her up with lots of things, which, I understand, included his furniture and car, his new skeleton crew, himself as Captain and someone who went with them for the sail.

The usual routine, before setting sail, meant that the boat had to be inspected and checked for safety by the exciseman, or whatever such a man is called. His orders were that the boat was overloaded, and the car and some other goods had to come off to lighten her, being such an old boat. Sadly, however, the owner/Captain disobeyed his orders and, so the story goes, returned all back on board before sailing.

The sail, we understood, was up the English coast, keeping near to the shore. This was likely as none were experienced seamen. Halfway up, a nasty storm arose with a very sad ending, our dear Lochinvar sank with all on board drowned, and only the top of the mast showing to mark the spot. It took quite some time before the bodies were washed ashore at different places, some quite a distance from the spot where the ship sank. The Captain's father had to go south several times to identify the bodies as they came ashore, his own son being one of the last.

The Lochaline Pier was a fairly new building, with two comfortable waiting rooms and large stores, but sadly lacked a fireplace, and so it could be very cold in winter. So the generous and kind piermaster and his wife, known fondly as Duncan and Peggy, had an open door for the older travellers if the steamer was late. The waiting at times could be very cheery, and the time soon passed. I remember a missioner assistant to our minister, very important in his own estimation, saying to a boy:

"Well, my little boy, and what are you going to be when you grow up?" The boy's answer being: "I am going to be a missionary, as it's a lazy job!" This, the child must have heard at home. I had a special warmth for the Lochinvar, as she came on the run, new, in 1907, the year I was born.

Yet another extremely sad ending, even more so than that of our dear Lochinvar, was that of our beautiful, largest and most graceful seasonal sailing ship, the Grenadier by name. She sailed daily to Iona, 6 days a week, as in the past no Sunday sailings were made, it being the correct thing to do to honour our God-given day of rest. Today, it seems to be a thing of the past, and Sunday being with most people, their busiest day of the week – all because of man's greed. Speaking for myself, we are all losers in so many ways.

The Grenadier would leave Oban, crowded, each day, generally in lovely sunshine, such as our summer weather was in the past. A lone dulcimer also joined the Grenadier for the season, playing almost all day. So, by the end of the season, he must have had a nice nest egg to tide him through the winter. It seems that the Grenadier had had the same Captain for years, retiring at a late age, well after the general time. The season following, he came back to Oban and sailed daily as a passenger, living on board. On her last sailing day of the season, she docked as usual at her Oban pier when, during the night, the watchman discovered a fire on board. Although the alarm was raised immediately, the fire spread so rapidly it was impossible to save her and, if I remember rightly, two men perished in their sleeping berths.

It was a dreadful tragedy; the young men looking out of their small porthole windows and asking those on the pier to shoot them. Everyone was so helpless, as the whole ship was ablaze. It was said afterwards, that the fire must have been started by the old Captain as he wasn't quite himself, and devoted to the ship as, although on the pier and safe, he ran back on board into the flames, and perished with her.

In my mind's eye, after all those many years, I can still see the Grenadier's long, graceful, streamlining, with the full-length figure of a lady on her bow.

On the subject of ships, I must relate a story that amused me and many others. It is said there is a vast difference between goody, goody, and being good, one must judge for oneself. Occasionally, in summer, one sees a liner anchored in the Sound of Mull, her motor launch taking passengers ashore. Previous to the war years, they were more frequent. One such liner visited Tobermory for the summer before the start of the war. Not having her own motor launch, the Lochinvar acted as tender, taking her passengers ashore. Now Tobermory, like any other small town, had an Italian shop which kept open on Sundays, paying their fine on Mondays in court. Also, at this time, there was a goody, goody lady with a similar shop, both sold post cards. The lady, so the story goes, never opened her shop on Sundays, but sold all her post cards to the Italian on Saturdays, who sold them to the passengers on Sundays.

Tobermory was a very busy Naval training base during the war, all ships having a stay of three weeks. Apart from our own British ships, there were also many from our friendly nations. Commodore Stevenson was in charge for the whole duration of the war, and a really smart, strict and just Commodore he was. Many were the amusing tales told of his training methods with the men, who always had to be very alert. Great was the praise he got for the smart ships that left Tobermory at the end of the three weeks' training.

Among the Naval personnel stationed at the base, such as staff on the Commodore's ship, in the Paymaster's Office, and all Naval repair men, were generally those men, who after a spell of duty at sea in the Navy, were brought to Tobermory for a peaceful rest break.

Richard Baker, who I generally listen to on Radio Two for his Sunday musical hour, had been a Middie, this being what the young trainee officers were called. These young men, if I remember correctly, trained for long spells, working on the Commodore's ship, and in later years, Richard wrote a book on his stay in Tobermory. It was a jolly good and interesting book, especially on life in the ship, with some very amusing stories and many interesting pictures. The Commodore, an old man, now retired and a friend of Richard, helped a lot at the time of his writing the book. Now, my writing of these days has reminded me that I had loaned my copy of the book to someone, but I have no recollection of who it was. As often happens, my book was never returned, yet today that book would be priceless to me in writing of those days.

During the early years of the war when, Clydebank was bombed, my late sister, married with two small boys, rented from friends a very nice house on the hill in Tobermory. It had 2 public and 3 bedrooms, garage and garden with a lovely open view over the Sound of Mull, and was to have been her home for some years to come.

Sadly, the dreadful tragedy of Clydebank brought about many changes, one being that the Campbells asked my sister to look for another house as Mrs. Campbell was so afraid of staying in Glasgow. Mr. Campbell was a Captain, and sailed from Glasgow weekly with his eldest son with him as mate, and docked each Saturday at Glasgow for the weekend, also, with his daughter teaching in Glasgow, they had a flat there as their home. Meanwhile, Mrs. Campbell stayed on in Tobermory until their youngest son finished his schooling there, when my sister was delighted to move into their house until such time as the Captain retired.

Houses were very difficult to come by at the time, so my sister and her husband, having looked over the Clydesdale Bank and bank house, on sale at the time, asked me if I could go over and help them decide, for if they bought the property, my sister would require my help and that of others besides. After much thought they put in an offer to buy, having decided that while she would require my help if successful, a local teenager would help mother. So the property became theirs, which meant them moving down to the main street and having to face plenty of hard work, both in the house and bank with its large counters and all other furnishings to be removed.

Once in to the bank house, and with two good friends gladly come to help us, we four working with a will, and plenty of joking and laughter, soon had the living quarters spick and span. Then came the task of starting on the bank-manager's office, with its huge furniture, bookcases and counters. The problem started when, looking for tradesmen to help us, we discovered that they were out on the Isle of Tiree, building at the aerodrome for the airbase there.

Here, the good Lord came to our rescue again. Answering the doorbell, I saw a tall, well-dressed, strange man looking for accommodation. Horrified, I said that we wished we could help, and asked who sent him. On getting the information, I opened the door wide and bowed as I welcomed him to step inside. He was a plumber from Nairn whose business had been taken over by the Navy to do all the plumbing work at the Tobermory Distillery, as it was being done out for the Naval personnel for the duration of the war. True to his word, he was God sent, for when he heard how we were placed, he said:

"You take me in and you won't regret it, as I will help you all I can."

Apart from being a thorough gent, and working hard for us, he also brought the carpenter off the Commodore's ship and other men as required. So it ended up that the work was done much better, and in less time, than the locals would have done. When the men came home for the weekend from Tiree, they said the work of clearing out would take at least a fortnight, so there was no point in working on a Saturday, but to wait until the Tiree work was ended. The naval men did the work in a matter of days, even though the bank floor was sagging because of the heavy counters, meaning that the floors had to be lifted and the foundations renewed.

Our next thought, as the place was being put in order, was how we were to furnish it, as coupons were required for everything. We did not need to worry for long, as the good Lord was on our side again. Looking through the daily Scotsman, my brother-in-law's favourite paper, for the chance of furniture sales, there, in Murrayfield Gardens, next door to friends, we saw a private house sale with a lot of what we required. So we contacted our friends who said I should go through immediately. We got very little out of the house, as relatives were bidding very high, but the little we got was of good quality.

I was asked to stay until we got all that was required, and apart from the furnishings, the carpenter had taken the measurements of all the carpets needed. We didn't have long to wait, as within a few days there was a sale in a large private house which had been closed for some time. Here we got 12 beautiful red Morocco leather dining chairs, on castors, most comfortable to sit on. I cannot remember what else we got. Next, we went to a fairly new hotel out in the country, and known as the Pantelles. Out of the last two places, we got all that we required.

All the hotel furnishing was as-new, as it had gone bankrupt. This furniture had been made by Taylors, and what we got there was marvellous. Six grand dining room tables, extra large size to seat four, with the top felts tailored into them – I've never seen their equal. The carpets were so thick, and with the stair carpet we got thick brass rods and hooks. We also bought one lot of the good china, but that was stolen and in its place was left a box of, more or less, useless things, but, in the end, the house was better furnished than had there not been a war on.

Our friend, Grandpa Angus, went with me to all the sales, so I gave him all the credit. He saw to everything, storing it all at his own premises. First he filled his garage, empty until the war would end, then all that he could squeeze into the house and his office in Frederick Street – even in the front office, much to the amusement of all who entered.

I then made my way back as quickly as possible, to get on with the work, while Grandpa Angus got all collected and sent up in a container.

Eventually, all the hard work was ended, and Tina, my sister, went with the boys to Ardtornish to see our parents, the eldest boy having started school. I also intended spending the week-end quietly, with only my brother-in-law, Archie, and Mr. Fraser, the plumber. Alas, our peaceful rest was rudely disturbed by the ringing of the door bell, which we at first ignored, as I was not very presentable, being in my dressing gown and my hair in curlers. So Archie, very much to his annoyance, had to answer the first time and what a shock as he walked in, pulling faces, followed by four high-ranking officers, to inspect the whole place, as the house was to be taken over for WRENS, soon to be stationed in Tobermory. There was the local Commodore Stevenson, Commander Palmer and two other officers from Greenock, one a medical officer. Even the outside premises were thoroughly inspected, after which one of them said: "Splendid, Even the sheds are as clean as the drawing room." Some drawing room, I thought, our humble lounge being minus of any of the drawing room valuables.

This was a dreadful shock to us, after all our hard work and expense, so, fight on we would as another, larger house, in its own grounds, on the hill was for sale. Our solicitor, who was good, and knew us well, agreed but advised us to take in some Naval personnel for the duration, so that saved us. We were discussing the matter when Commander Palmer called to say he wished to bring his wife to stay, preferably to the Western Isles Hotel.

It was very essential that we had some time to ourselves before opening the house to the Naval personnel, and we were also having Grandpa Angus for a well-deserved holiday, after his great kindness to us. Alas, once more our restful spell was denied us. The Provost, a bachelor in his late thirties living with his mother, was getting married, and he wanted the reception to be held at our place, which was a bit ridiculous, as the house was not that big. So when the bride and her sister called, the answer was definitely no, but they persisted. So thinking back to when I was only 19 years old and forced to shoulder the responsibility at Dundas, I thought why not, if they agreed on the small number our dining room could take. Johnnie, the Provost, being a licensed grocer, said he would supply any-thing we required, overlooking food being rationed, so we agreed, as my sister was also friendly with Johnnie's family. It was made clear, never again, Johnnie's wedding would be our first and last.

Fortunately we took Grandpa up from Edinburgh, after our quiet weekend, on getting the place in order, which turned out not to be quiet, as I have written. He was in his mid-seventies, with a heart problem, so Tina said I should go to Oban and meet him off the train. This was his first visit to Tobermory, and he enjoyed himself greatly, but the poor old dear was rather a nuisance as he would not go out on his own, Tina or I having to go with him.

After Tina's first walk with him, she said: "Please, Agnes, will you take on the job, as I don't seem to have the talk, and you know him so much better." So twice daily, I was seen out, and Tobermory, being a small town, and no different from any other for gossip, it came back to us that I was being lamented. Such a young girl throwing herself away marrying such an old man, even if he was a nice gentleman. Among ourselves this was a grand joke, which we did not deny. Of course with our slow walk, because of his heart condition, and his wearing the now old-fashioned spats, he looked more like eighty. Today, even at eighty, he would be too young for me, now 86 years old.

Now, me being the old-fashioned one, and showing a niece a fur hat I was very proud of, she said, with a strange look: "Since it's warm that's the main thing." The hat was bought recently by a friend, lately come to live here from England, to defy our cold winters. Being on the small side and not suiting her, it was laughed at by her family, which suited me so I became the lucky owner.

In planning the wedding feast, and every other thing it entailed, we were again most fortunate. Where was all the china, glasses and cutlery to be got for 36 guests? Our good friends came to the rescue, and with plenty of flower vases as well as offered help for the big day, thereby getting us off to a good start. With Grandpa's holiday over, and friends taking the two boys out of the way, I was locked in the kitchen, "wonder of wonders," with a chef and two good, hard-working, friends. Tina was in the dining room serving, with our two good friends who had helped with the cleaning of the house.

First, how we came to have the good fortune of the chef who, more or less, took over from me, was another of the good Lord's surprises to us. He was chef on one of the corvettes, just come up for training, and was married to the Ardtornish keeper's daughter, who he met when chef in the Gleneagles Hotel and she was receptionist. Looking across from Tobermory to Morvern, he questioned how he could get to Morvern on his off-duty time, and was advised to come to us, being from Morvern.

Cash being scarce with us meant we spent wisely, and Archie, being purser on the wee Lochinvar, bought a box of fish from the fish-wife's barrow, my task being to fillet them. This I was doing at the kitchen sink when Tina, answering the door bell, returned with this nice, tall, cheery young Naval Petty Officer. Coming over to the sink, he said: "I'll do that for you."

Thinking he was joking, I said: "If you could, you would not be so generous."

"Try me," he said.

So I handed over my knife. Gosh, I was stunned – he could fillet three to my one!

There was our chef, who spent all his off-duty with us in the kitchen. We filled all the large biscuit tins with meringues and all that could be prepared beforehand for the big day.

On the wedding day he got early leave, for unbelievably the corvette, having finished training, was leaving Tobermory very early the next morning. Arthur, as he was called, was a real Godsend, making the wedding feast a great success, everything going like clockwork, and food being passed through the hatch we had got made when the office was being converted into a dining room. With our helpers serving with Tina, there was as much joking and laughter as when cleaning. Hence, from start to finish, it was a happy, jolly wedding, with hours spent in the dining room when the tables were cleared, as all were cheery, but far from having indulged too much.

Mrs. Sharpe, one of our good friends who served in the dining room, was a real comedian who, as always, started the fun going along with one of the men guests, a great actor. Although Johnnie, the bridegroom, gave a dance to the town, it was a disappointment to start with, as the fun in the dining room kept the party from the town hall opening with people never noticing how quick the time was passing.

With the war on, and travelling more difficult, most of the guests were local, and each knowing the other, helped to make it such a happy time. When the party eventually went to the dance hall, some of the happy couple's friends took the chance of getting into their bedroom to play lots of tricks, as the couple were spending the night with us before going south first thing in the morning.

I never realised what I was letting myself in for when we agreed to the reception, forgetting that all carving was done by the butler at Dundas, so Arthur's help was a double blessing, being so well trained. He had even worked abroad, one place being King Farok of Egypt's yacht.

Apart from Commander and Mrs. Palmer, we decided we would take in the younger lower-rank men as they would be less trouble and would live with ourselves, using our lounge and kitchen for meals, they being birds of passage having restful duty after their spell at sea. Commander Palmer, like the Commodore, both elderly men, were in Tobermory for the duration of the war. I made the mistake of calling the Commodore Commander, when first mentioning him. We were also open daily for officers' afternoon tea, for those men who preferred our quiet place to the licensed Western Isle Hotel.

It was a very wise decision taking in the Petty Officers, as they were a marvellous help, and all four, being such nice lads, made our place a real home, helping in every way when off-duty. This was especially so as, unfortunately, I was taken twice, as a stretcher case, to Oban Hospital.

The first time was with a carbuncle on my face – what I called my war medal. The flesh has filled in now, although for a long time it felt like I only had half a face. I was in a bad state, as with it being so near my ear, the pus was getting into my ear and everywhere, and I could do nothing being so heavily bandaged, especially at night. With four boils, the nurses, although very busy, had to clean my face almost constantly.

Next was my perforated duodenum ulcer, the cause of me being exempt when called up. Those Petty Officers were a tower of strength to my sister. Never would they leave her when off-duty, even joining her and the boys for evening church, where Archie was an Elder. Each wrote to me daily, in turn, so I was well supplied with letters full of nonsense, apart from all the news, to cheer me, and the same applied to the phone. Each, when on duty in the office, at 9 p.m. would take turns, and talking such nonsense, that they caused great excitement among the nurses and caused such a scamper to see who could get to the phone first when the shout went up Sunny Boy. The cause of the rush was when the nurses asked their name, and one said Sunny Boy, this lad was forever laughing, hence his nickname.

Eventually, the nurses were so excited over the letters, that they would open and read them to me, they certainly cheered up the hospital. The house, being on the main street, the door bell was so handy, folk passing would ring to ask after me, which was rather a nuisance to my sister, when so busy in the mornings. To the amusement of all, one of the lads had a bright idea to help her – he would pin a small bulletin on the door. "A splendid idea," said Tina, "but it could offend our kind friends."

Now in spite of our saying no more weddings, and being so busy, two more girls came wanting us to hold their reception, the first, being Johnnie's sister, a teacher. This was unbelievable when there were two hotels on the main street, the Mishnish at one end, the Macdonald Arms at the other.

Sadly, on returning to duty at sea, we heard that two of our lads were lost with their ships, yet, on a cheery and amusing note, two others arrived safely in Australia. It was Sunny Boy's laughter that brought them together at some Naval entertainment. Even now, at my bedside, I have a lambskin rug that one of the lads sent to my sister from Australia.

It has just come to mind that I was rushed to Oban Hospital, by lifeboat, some years previously, caused by my duodenum ulcer. On slowly coming to, which must have been a Sunday afternoon, I wondered where I was, Hearing a strange noise, I just lay quietly, then my tummy reminded me that I was in hospital, and the noise was the patter of many feet – so the floor covering must have been lino. Suddenly, I did come full circle, hearing the visitor with the patient next to me questioning who I was. Her answer – The sister-in-law of the crabbed purser on the Lochinvar. I felt like laughing out loud and opening my eyes, to let them know that I had heard and to see who the visitor was, thinking she must have been one who travelled cabin on a steerage ticket.

Now the Lochinvar, being small, was usually crowded, and many were the complaints sent to the head shipping office in Glasgow from cabin passengers unable to get a seat, caused by steerage passengers cheating. All those letters were sent back to Archie, who had to check once all the tickets had been issued, and so out of the cabin the cheats had to go. People travelling to Oban were, generally, all locals and all knowing each other, gents and workers alike, and the one who enjoyed the joke most was Archie.

Tobermory certainly was a busy little town as a Naval base, with everyone who was free and able, doing their bit to entertain the fleet as the ships came and went for training. The best at this being the minister's wife, Mrs. Menzies, a marvellous and clever entertainer. She suggested that we must try to get round as many of the lads as possible, which meant inviting different ones each week. Alas, as she shook hands and bid them all goodnight, she was greatly thanked, and asked if they could return the next time, so, of course, she had not the heart to refuse them during their stay. She also opened the Manse laundry for any of the personnel, wives or men, to use, and much more besides.

She was also the church organist, and now widowed, it was nice for them both that she had her only child, a daughter, very comfortably married beside her in Tobermory. When, one afternoon, she failed to turn up at church, the daughter, going to see the cause, very, very sadly found her dead from a heart attack in the bath. She was mourned by all who knew her – this being shortly after the war.

Mrs. Palmer, the Commander's wife, was Muriel Cracknel, a famous singer, but never known to us or anyone else in the Highlands, until she came to stay with us. She, too, was a very nice friendly lady who did her bit by singing at the entertainments. I can still see her in my mind's eye, singing The Holy City.

The autumn after my nasty ulcer operation, she took me down on holiday to her home, on a hill in Kent, "Cold Blowhouse", a lovely place with such a huge orchard and a swimming pool in the centre. If I remember correctly, she had couple of pigs in, from a farmer, to eat the fallen fruit, especially the apples. Their two boys were home from training, having finished at boarding school. One was for the Navy, like his Dad, but I cannot remember what the other did, although for several years after the war, at Christmas, my sister and I were sent a leaflet book with separate pictures of all four, each with information about all their news and doings. Then we had one picture of all four of them together, and a poem by the Commander. I had endless pictures, verses and lovely drawing in an autograph book, all war memories, but once in my eighties, I handed all over to my young relations.

As many of we working class found out, it took a long time to put a home together but, alas, a short time to scatter, when it seemed such a short time to have enjoyed.

However once again our comfort. "Lay up treasures in Heaven that faileth not. Where no thief approacheth, neither moth corrupteth, for where our treasures are there will our hearts be also."

Of course furniture, all antique, and other large articles, I divided between Erskine Hospital and the war blinded hospital on the outskirts of Edinburgh, whose name I have at present forgotten. All were gladly given in grateful appreciation for so many young men sacrificing most of their lives for the country and us. This I know, having visited both hospitals, with a feeling of great sadness.

Still on the war years, my brother, bringing his bride home to us on her first visit, on leaving London the bombing started and so they had to seek shelter. My brother, thinking sure he had the truth, said that once up north in Scotland, you will scarcely know there is a war on, and certainly won't lose a night's sleep.

Little did he know. As the evening train was getting into Oban, the sirens went off and a bomb, or bombs, were dropped on a convoy of ships in the Firth of Lorn, this being the spot where they always gathered before setting sail abroad, to whatever destination they were bound. The memory of the full story has left me, but what I do remember was a bomb dropped on a ship taking race horses to America. All seemed to have gone down with the ship except for one who, somehow, broke loose enabling him to swim ashore, landing near Connel, where he was found next morning contentedly grazing, dragging his broken reins.

Another sad story was when a convoy, nearing its journey's end and laden with its precious and much-needed load, was coming, in line, through the Sound of Mull opposite Craignure, and one of the ships was seen to be sinking. Nothing could be done to save it, having been scuttled by a spy on board. No lives were lost, and the spy, gladly, was caught. That sunken ship from time to time up until the present, I understand is used to train men for diving.

One young Tobermory lad, at the time for his calling up for service, when offered diving training on the ship, being near his home gladly accepted and did very well. Eventually, after the war, he was in charge of diving on some of the ships lost near our coasts.

Once, when his younger brother who was also at sea but currently on leave getting married, was told by his brother that if he wished to make arrangements to miss one voyage, he could join him on the salvage ship. Having been given permission to miss the voyage, he happily joined his brother for the work. Sadly, a dreadful tragedy descended on that nice family, who we knew very well.

Neil, the youngest son, in Oban High School, and his mother, Mrs. McQuarrie, a widow, seemed to have all going well for them when Neil took ill in school and was sent back to his lodgings. A doctor was called who decided he be sent to hospital, Neil admitting that he had felt ill for some time but did not like to complain, being from home. His health deteriorated, and his mother was sent for, arriving shortly before

Neil passed away. It was such a terrible sadness for her, having to return home with his body, but much worse was to follow before the flowers had faded on Neil's sacred ground. The local police received word to go and break the awful news to Mrs. McQuarrie that there had been an explosion on the ship her sons worked on, killing one son and injuring the other, who was now in hospital.

The police, unable to break such news, decided that the best person was a recently retired minister, my uncle by marriage. At the time the daily papers contained dreadful news of a murderer. I remember it well, but not the name.

Allowing a certain time to pass after the second burial, my sister and I went to see Mrs. McQuarrie. She seemed so very calm, and told us she had received such wonderful comfort from Uncle John. On getting her to sit down beside him, he explained that he was the bearer of sad news, but first she was to understand that he could have been the bearer of so much worse – that her son was a murderer, such as was then being read about – but he had come to tell her that her son had died a noble death for his country. She then compared both cases and found a wonderful peace of thankfulness from God which eased her pain.

Now back to the 1914 war, when suitable horses were all rounded up and taken. Mr. C. Sellar, having a race horse he was very fond of, decided that it was not going to be taken. So he took poor Peking to a nice place by his favourite walk and there had him shot, sewn in sheets, and buried along with the silver cups he had won. How many cups were buried with the horse I do not know but it could only have been about two. I doubt today the cups would have stayed buried there for long if people knew the spot. For myself, I don't think Mr. Sellar did the right thing, for what would have happened if all the people had done the same thing? I have no recollection if he sent any other of his horses, but I suppose he must have done.

Another 1914 war memory. When I was very young, we were often sent out from school to gather sphagnum moss for the hospitals, this being used for wounds. The moss was very plentiful and easily gathered, growing so clean in damp ground. It held water like a sponge, which we squeezed out and spread the moss out to dry in the air on clean sheets. When perfectly dry, we picked out any strings of grass growing through it, and then, being extremely light, it was easily packed.

Last summer, for the first time, I got the chance to be taken on a motor outing through miles of forestry ground, by the man in charge, who was going to check on trees having to be cut down. What surprises I got that saddened me very much. I never realised such work, or damage, was caused through the planting of trees. The woodland life we used to enjoy as children was all gone, everything in the thick woods was dead, all except the endless trees, even the animal and bird life had gone. What a fearful, crushing, painful, silence – no movement, no life. The endless plants of all types, such as the wild orchids and scented shrubs, had vanished. When we were young we could not afford fresh flowers to plant or have in the house, but they were never missed as we never went without the beautiful flowers that grew wild – carpets of speedwells, blue-bells, primroses, iris, etc. All I managed to find, as my companion attended to his work, was a tiny patch of sphagnum moss.

My companion showed me how all the woods had to be drained for the trees to grow. The drains were dug so many feet deep, with the sides in some places being cemented for fear of them falling in and, at the same time, the bottom of the drains were filled with tons of gravel. All this expense to keep the drains running clear, thereby keeping the ground almost parched. I thought to myself that the trees would need to pay well in the end.

The Englishman, I'd say in his forties, when he had finished his work and we were leaving the forest, asked what I had been gathering. He had neither seen or heard of spagnum moss, but was very interested when I told him all I knew about it. Once I had dried the very little I had found, and it likely being the last, I intended keeping it, but decided to let him have it. So he put it in a clear plastic bag and, being very proud of it, keeps it on show in his lounge.

No wonder I say that life has completely changed since my childhood days. Progress and chemicals have destroyed God's priceless gifts to us.

Three weeks ago the making, in Tobermory, of the film "I Know Where I Am Going", with Wendy Hillier as the actress, was shown at 10.20 p.m. This, I think, was shortly before the war years, and how we old folks, still alive, especially in Tobermory, looked forward to reviving precious memories. Although I was not in Tobermory at the time, I spent quite a lot of my life there during the war years.

Nowadays, I go to bed by 6 o'clock, after supper, generally in time to listen to the 6 o'clock news and read, but this particular night I was up and out to my good neighbour at 10 o'clock, not wanting to miss it. I, myself, never, never have the TV on, as I hear many other old folk don't either, it being so different in the past when we thoroughly enjoyed many fine things shown.

What a disappointment. It was, more or less, only snippets that were shown. The only voice I recognised was that of our good friend, Mrs. Sharpe ("Polly"), witty as usual and still very much alive. It was so nice being brought back to memory, as we old folk are, when our travelling days are over, often inclined to forget our friends until something jogs the memory – as this did with me. So I said to myself: "Next evening, Agnes, you phone Polly."

She answered quite smartly, her voice still strong. "Hallo, dear," came through.

"Now, Polly, I could be an enemy" – laughter – everyone is dear to me. We then had a happy chat, with me telling her that all I remembered of the film was the scenery and her voice, and how on earth was she dressed up in that fashion?

It seems that Wendy Hillier had had a day off, so Polly was asked to stand in for her, dressed up in Wendy's togs with a large floppy hat, no wonder I did not recognise her. It was when the producer said to Polly, as she raced to shelter from a shower: "I am pleased to see you taking care of Wendy's £90 hat," that Polly's voice rang out: "£90, well, if I've never had £90 in my hands, I can always say that I had £90 on my head."

I daresay Polly was as beautiful as the actress, good looking, handsome, and with a joyous, lovely nature, admired by all who knew her and, as I found out, still her old self. She will be 90 years old in May, if spared, and she told me that it is only within the past year she has felt herself failing. However, I'm glad to think she isn't too bad as yet, for when I phoned, she had been waiting for a friend to take her to a whist drive. She, like myself, realises God has greatly blessed her.

Another short, interesting, and surprising happening to me. I visit my only sister regularly, and have been for the past 5 years, come May. She is well cared for in every way, as are all with her. There are about 12 patients, I think, in a small, independent ward, private and on its own. It does not at all, look like a hospital, except for the nurses uniforms. I must mention that it was my sister's 90th birthday last week, and what a lovely time and party the nurses gave her, dressing her up specially for the occasion – as they do all their patients. In January they had a very, very special celebration, the eldest patient reaching her 101st birthday, with endless cards, over 100, many gifts, and beautiful flowers, filling and beautifying their already nice, comfortable lounge.

On this particular day, a small, smart lady came over to me with outstretched hands saying: 'You are Agnes Robertson, I knew you when a child. You are now 86 and I am 96. Your parents' farm bordered ours and your parents had to move as your other two sisters had come of age for school, and no school being near the farm."

What a memory! It was as clear as a bell. She had still been living at her home, alone, until some months ago, when she took shingles on her head. She was taken to hospital where, on recovering, the wise doctors kept her, even though she was anxious to get home to her lovely pussies which she missed so much.

She seems to be well supplied with good-quality, tailored, smart fitted dresses, all made by herself from patterns she had bought, also jewellery of different kinds. Like me, and many others, she does not like TV, and so spends quite some time in her bedroom with her nice belongings beside her.

She had heard of me through my sister and the nurses, as she always seems to be talking about Mull. Coming many years ago, with her late sister, to retire to Oban, but at a different end from us, of course we never knew anything about them.

With what joy and thankfulness I see myself nearing the last page of the jotter, doubting at times if I could do so. So I must end by telling of a happening to myself when very young, I think 5 or 6 years old, and not very complimentary I fear. For some strange reason it keeps returning to jog my memory this past few days, after such a lifetime, and seems very clear. I was very upset and, try as I will, the reason will not become clear, only that it happened at home and not at school. I wanted to fight back as I was so angry, but could not do so. That day, in school, I remember we were all given a hyacinth bulb to plant, to be returned when in bloom for prizes to be awarded. I took my bulb home, and with my two, small, white hands, tore it in bits getting, I remember, comfort in doing so. Then, as I looked at it all in shreds, all anger vanished, then came a sadness, so clear to me as I write this. It taught me a lesson I never forgot.

Now today, nearing my life's end, I look at and study those same hands, dainty, white ones no more, but plain, ordinary, and hard working. I think over my long life and once again say: "Thank You Lord."

When our best beloved sister passed away, and with a brother overwhelmed with grief, I was wondering how I could help when a clear, silent voice said: "Write something."

On taking out my hymn book, 3rd edition, I opened it at the centre page and was surprised to see the printing larger than I ever saw before. The words seemed new to me, but ever so suitable, so I copied them all then put the book to one side, open, to study when I had more time, but all the words had vanished. I mentioned this to an old, retired, choir friend, surprising her also but, she said, one poem in an old book was similar.

## The Golden Chain

Whither, pilgrims, are you going?

We are going on a journey, going to a better land.

Fear ye not the way so lonely, you a little feeble band?

No; for friends unseen are near us, Christ, our leader walks beside us,

He will guard and He will guide us, guide us to the better land.

Tell us pilgrims, what you hope for in that far off better land?

Spotless robes and crowns of glory from a Saviours loving hand.

We shall drink of life's clear river, we shall dwell with Christ forever,

In that bright and better land.

Pilgrims, may we travel with you to that bright and better land?

Come and welcome, come and welcome, welcome to our pilgrim band,

Come, O come, and do not leave us; God is waiting to receive us,

In that bright and better land.


Christian life, pilgrimage and rest.
For Ron, from Agnes, June 12th, 1990.

## God's Wonderful Miracle

I live in the main door flat of a large tenement with a garden and raised plots on either side of the 6 steps to the entrance. On the top step, a friend left a plastic bag of dried manure and 12 lovely pansy plants he had grown from seed. Being out when he called, and coming in tired, I decided to leave them until morning. Getting up at 6.30 a.m., and washed, dressed and having enjoyed my early-morning cup of tea, it being a lovely June morning, I then went out to plant the pansies. Having finished one border, I moved to the second, and finding I had forgotten a tool, I stepped out to collect it. Putting my right foot on the plastic bag, then lifting my left foot, the bag with my right foot on slipped. I remember being in mid-air, but not having landed on the road.

On coming to, with severe pains in my back and head, and completely blind, I said to myself: "Oh, Agnes, your end has come very suddenly." Then the silent, inward, clear voice said: "You live by faith, ask to be healed."

So I said: "Lord, you are the great physician, please heal me." The words were no sooner uttered when the pain from my back was completely gone, and partially gone from my head. I seemed to be coming alive, with my eyesight slowly returning.

This being early morning, before the traffic started moving, when I was able to move, I called a neighbour who phoned a doctor. Then it was off to hospital where, to the surprise of those about, no broken bones showed up on the X-ray, nor again after spending 10 days in hospital, and also no ill effects. "The Marvellous Miracle."

I had my eyesight completely returned, and although the

large lump on my head had burst and bled for all day it, too,
healed up perfectly.

Who would doubt God's existence?

## Psalm 15

Within thy tabernacle, Lord,
    Who shall abide with thee,
And in thy high and holy hill
    Who shall a dweller be?

The man that walketh uprightly,
    And worketh righteouness,
And as he thinketh in his heart,
    So doth he truth express.

Who doth not slander with his tongue,
    Nor to his friend doth hurt;
Nor yet against his neighbour doth
    Take up an ill report.

In whose eyes vile men are despised;
    But those that God do fear
He honoureth; and changes not,
    Though to his hurt he swear.

His coin puts not to usury,
    Nor take reward will he
Against the guiltless, who doth thus
    Shall never moved be.

## *By Albert Frederick Bayly*

O Lord of every shining constellation
That wheels in splendour through the midnight sky;
Grant us thy Spirit's true illumination
To read the secrets of thy work on high.

And thou who mad'st the atom's hidden forces,
Whose laws its mighty energies fulfil;
Teach us, to whom thou giv'st such rich resources,
In all we use, to serve thy holy will.

O Life, awaking life in cell and tissue,
From flower to bird, from beast to brain of man;
O help us trace, from birth to final issue,
The sure unfolding of thine ageless plan.

Thou who hast stamped thine image on thine creatures,
And though they marred that image lov'st them still;
Uplift our eyes to Christ, that in his features
We may discern the beauty of thy will.

Great Lord of nature, shaping and renewing,
Who mad'st us more than nature's sons to be;
Help us to tread, with grace our souls enduring,
The road to life and immortality.

## My Special Prayer

My God, accept my heart this day
 And make it always thine,
That I from thee no more may stray,
 No more from thee decline.

Before the cross of Him who died,
 Behold, I prostrate fall;
Let every sin be crucified
 And Christ be all in all.

Anoint me with thy heavenly grace,
 And seal me for thine own;
That I may see thy glorious face,
 And worship near thy throne.

Let every thought and work and word
 To thee be ever given;
Then life shall be thy service, Lord,
 And death the gate of Heaven.

All glory to the Father be,
 All glory to the Son,
All glory Holy Ghost, to thee,
 While endless ages run.

Amen